Poland

Poland

BY WIL MARA

Enchantment of the World™
Second Series

CHILDREN'S PRESS®

An Imprint of Scholastic Inc.

New York Toronto London Auckland Sydney
Mexico City New Delhi Hong Kong
Danbury, Connecticut

Frontispiece: **Market Square, Wroclaw**

Consultant: M. B. B. Biskupski, Professor of History, Central Connecticut State University, New Britain, Connecticut
Please note: All statistics are as up-to-date as possible at the time of publication.

Book production by The Design Lab

Library of Congress Cataloging-in-Publication Data
Mara, Wil.
 Poland / by Wil Mara.
 pages cm. — (Enchantment of the world)
 Includes bibliographical references and index.
 ISBN 978-0-531-22016-0 (lib. bdg.)
 1. Poland—Juvenile literature. I. Title.
 DK4040.M37 2014
 943.8—dc23   2013026061

All rights reserved. Published in 2014 by Children's Press, an imprint of Scholastic Inc.
Printed in the United States of America 141
SCHOLASTIC, CHILDREN'S PRESS, and associated logos are trademarks and/or registered trademarks of Scholastic Inc.

1 2 3 4 5 6 7 8 9 10 R 23 22 21 20 19 18 17 16 15 14

Traditional wooden carving

Contents

Left to right: **Red deer, bicyclist, acrobats, college students, Independence Day**

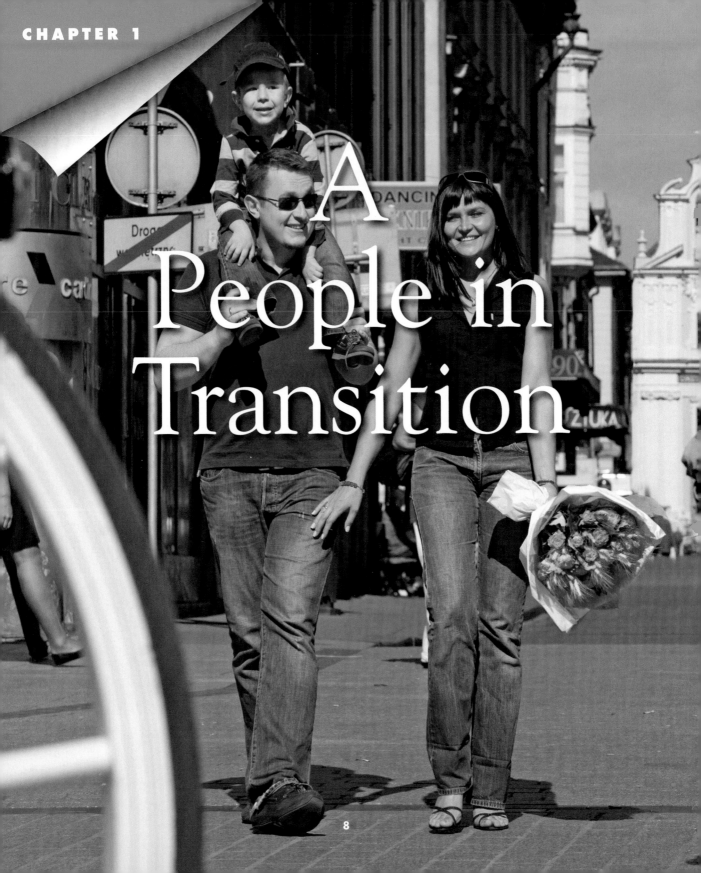

CHAPTER 1

A People in Transition

CELINA SITS AT HER KITCHEN TABLE PAYING LITTLE attention to her breakfast. Instead, she is staring out the apartment window, listening to a group of children playing in the empty lot below. She loves the sound of children playing and has dreamed all her life of having at least two of her own—one girl and one boy. Her parents had six, and her mother's parents had nine, so she comes from a long line of big families. But Poland was also a very different place back then.

Poland is a country in central Europe. Over the centuries, its borders have changed frequently—and sometimes disappeared entirely—but the Polish culture has endured.

Poland has experienced tremendous change during the lives of Celina's parents and grandparents. She has heard about the atrocities of World War II all her life. Germany invaded her homeland, and Adolf Hitler's Nazi regime slaughtered millions of Polish Jewish citizens. Millions of other

Opposite: **A family walks through the streets of Krakow. Most Polish families have only one child.**

non-Jewish Poles were killed or injured during the fighting. Barely a day went by when she didn't hear a story from one of her grandparents about the horrible events of World War II. No one in her family was Jewish, but they had friends who were—and by the war's end, every one of those friends was gone. Celina was born long after, but she has heard so much about it that she feels as if she lived through it.

After the war, Poland came under communist control. The government controlled the economy and owned most of the businesses. The Soviet Union, a large communist country to the east made up of Russia and neighboring regions, came to dominate Poland. The government of another land told Polish people how to live, what they could and couldn't do, could and couldn't say, could and couldn't think. Celina remembers her father complaining bitterly about this when she was a little girl. She remembers him coming home from his job at an automobile factory wearing his uniform and covered in sweat and grime. The Soviet government had assigned him the job, but he had no interest in it whatsoever. Her mother

Soviet troops enter Praga, near Warsaw, during World War II. Although the Soviet Union helped liberate Poland from German forces, it continued to dominate Poland for decades after the war ended.

Elderly Poles sit on a bench near Krasinski Palace in Warsaw. Poland has undergone dramatic changes during their lifetime.

would warn him to keep his voice low, as if there were people lingering by the windows to hear if he said anything against the Soviet leadership. As Celina later learned, her mother had good reason to be concerned—several people they knew were punished for speaking their mind. One couple was taken from their home during the night and never seen again.

People walk through a sunny square in Warsaw.

Celina was in elementary school during the time Poland gradually broke free of Soviet rule in the 1980s. Her history teacher was an older man who never used to smile, but he smiled a lot after that. So did her parents and her grandparents. In fact, so did just about every adult she knew. At the time, she didn't fully understand what had happened, but she could tell that it was something good.

As the years passed, she noticed how Poland changed. There were more stores to visit and more food on the shelves at the local supermarket. People seemed to have more money. She heard people talking about politics in public, and no one seemed scared.

Now, in the twenty-first century, she can look back on what has happened in Poland through the decades. She has a better understanding of the Poland of her grandparents, the

Shoppers choose from the abundant fresh produce at a market in Wroclaw. Poles have access to many more products and opportunities than they did just a few decades ago.

Poland of her parents, and the Poland that she will be inheriting. Poland has undergone dramatic changes in a brief time. She believes her parents and grandparents when they tell her life in Poland has never been as good as it is now. She sees all the exciting opportunities available.

Celina also knows her generation still faces challenges. Although she and her husband are earning more money than their parents did, everything costs a lot more, too. They are trying to save money so they can move out of their apartment and buy a house, but it is taking a lot longer than they thought it would. They also have to pay for health care and their pensions. They try to give some money to their local church, too, although her husband isn't happy about this. He says the church is too involved with the government, and he doesn't like supporting it. Her parents and grandparents never questioned what the church did, and she was raised to be the same way. But there are days when she understands her husband's point of view.

Overall, she feels good about the future of her country. She knows there will be many bright days ahead. She realizes Poland is a country in the midst of a transition, and she's trying to be patient and work through it like everyone else. She just wishes the transition would move a little faster. Maybe for those children outside, she thinks. Maybe everything will be perfect for them.

Then she realizes her parents and grandparents had thought the exact same thing about their children.

Girls dance to a traditional band in Krakow.

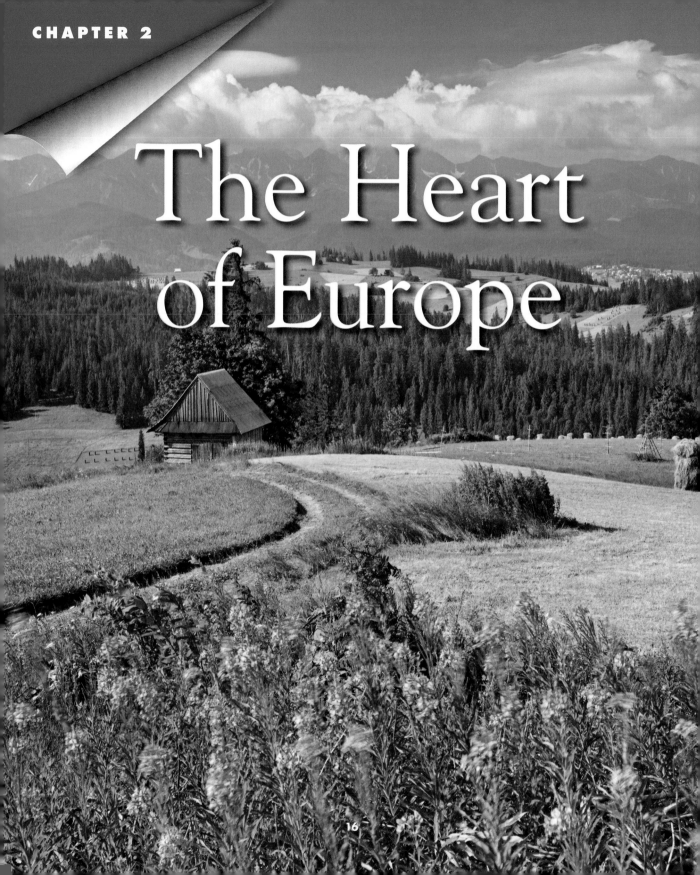

CHAPTER 2

The Heart of Europe

POLAND IS A ROUGHLY SQUARE-SHAPED COUNTRY that lies in central Europe. It is surrounded by seven other nations. Kaliningrad, a part of Russia that is separate from the rest of the country, lies to the extreme northeast. Along Poland's eastern border are Lithuania, Belarus, and Ukraine. To the south are Slovakia and the Czech Republic. And to the west lies Germany. The northern coast of Poland faces the Baltic Sea. Covering an area of 120,726 square miles (312,679 square kilometers), Poland is about the same size as the U.S. state of New Mexico. About 38,383,809 people live in Poland, making it the eighth most populous European nation.

Opposite: **A mix of forests and fields cover the mountains of southern Poland.**

The Lay of the Land

Most of Poland is flat land, a region commonly known as the Polish Plains. Part of the North European Plain, it rarely rises above 500 feet (150 meters). The only mountains in Poland are found in the southern part of the country. Within this broad outline, however, Poland can be divided into several regions.

Poland's Geographic Features

Area: 120,726 square miles (312,679 sq km)

Highest Elevation: Mount Rysy, 8,199 feet (2,499 m) above sea level

Lowest Elevation: Raczki Elblaskie in the Vistula Lagoon, 6 feet (1.8 m) below sea level

Longest River: Vistula, 651 miles (1,048 km)

Largest Lake: Sniardwy, 44 square miles (114 sq km)

Largest City: Warsaw, about 1.7 million people

Area with Greatest Rainfall: Valley of Five Lakes in the Tatra Mountains, 71 inches (180 cm) per year

Area with Least Rainfall: Kujawy, in central Poland, 12 inches (30 cm) per year

Average Daily High Temperature: In Warsaw, 30°F (–1°C) in January, 75°F (24°C) in July

Average Daily Low Temperature: In Warsaw, 21°F (–6°C) in January, 59°F (15°C) in July

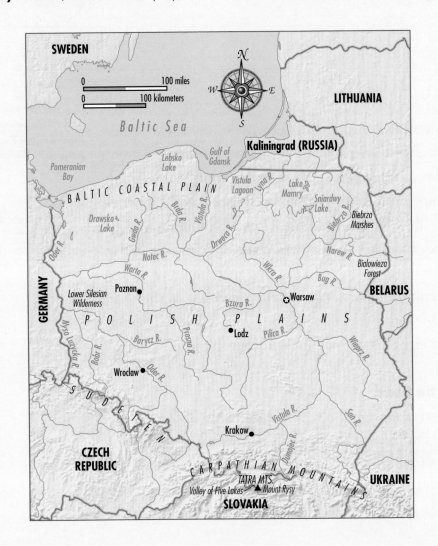

The Baltic Coastal Plain lies along the Baltic Sea in the extreme north. The coastline is fairly straight and uniform. The only major inlets are the Pomeranian Bay in the west and the Gulf of Gdansk in the east. It also features coastal lakes and lagoons, bodies of water that have been cut off from the sea by sandbars. Most of Poland's rivers flow into the Baltic Sea. The Polish government is working to protect the nation's wetland areas. More than a hundred wetland areas have been designated as national parks, wildlife reserves, or other protected regions.

Just to the south of the coastal plain is the lake region. This area is mostly flat, but there are several gently rising hills. Poland as a whole has more than nine thousand lakes, and most of them are in the lake region. Poland's largest lakes include Sniardwy, Lebsko, Drawsko, and Mamry, each of which covers more than 40 square miles (100 sq km). Today, many Polish people enjoy boating, parasailing, and water-skiing on many of these lakes.

Lake Mamry is a popular tourist destination. Sailboats can make their way from the lake through a canal to the Baltic Sea.

The sharp peaks of Mount Rysy are often shrouded in clouds.

Poland's largest region is the central lowlands. The region consists of flat plains broken up by lakes and rivers. Some of Poland's largest cities, including Warsaw and Lodz, are in this region.

The lesser Poland uplands lie just south of the central lowlands. This hilly region is rich in coal and other minerals such as iron, zinc, and lead.

The southern part of Poland is its mountainous region. The Carpathian Mountains rise along the southeastern border, extending into Ukraine, Slovakia, and beyond. The Tatra Range, part of the Carpathians, includes the highest point in Poland. Mount Rysy rises 8,199 feet (2,499 m) along the border between Poland and Slovakia. Another mountain range, called the Sudeten, crosses from southern Poland into the Czech Republic.

Almost all of the rivers in Poland flow into the Baltic Sea. The nation's two greatest rivers, the Vistula and the Oder, rise in the mountains south of Poland and then flow all the way across the country. The Vistula, Poland's longest river, flows for more than 651 miles (1,048 kilometers), ending in the Gulf of Gdansk. The Oder enters the Baltic farther west.

How's the Weather?

Poland lies in a temperate zone. This means that the climate is warm in the summer and cold in the winter. Summer temperatures tend to rise to 75 degrees Fahrenheit (24 degrees Celsius) or 80°F (27°C), with highs sometimes reaching the 90s and occasionally topping 100°F (38°C) in some southwestern areas. Winter temperatures are generally in the low to mid-30s Fahrenheit, although the coldest areas, located in the northeast, can dip lower.

Water, Water Everywhere

Some of Poland's worst natural disasters have been floods. One of the most devastating examples occurred over a five-day period in July 1934. During that time, record amounts of rain fell on a number of areas and caused several major rivers to swell and then surge over their banks, resulting in more than fifty deaths. In one valley region of the Tatra Mountains alone, about 10 inches (25 centimeters) of rain fell in a roughly twenty-four-hour period, submerging some homes so only the tops of the chimneys were visible. More recently, in July 2012 and again in April 2013, major floods toppled buildings, destroyed croplands, and tore up roadways.

A Look at Poland's Cities

With about 760,000 residents, Krakow (below) is Poland's second-largest city, trailing only the capital, Warsaw. It is located in the southern part of the country, in the lesser Poland uplands. Krakow is both a busy economic center and a cultural hub, with a lively academic community and artistic scene. It is one of Poland's oldest cities, having become a trade center in the tenth century and the capital of Poland in the eleventh century. Unlike many Polish cities, Krakow was not destroyed in World War II, and many of its historic buildings still stand. Its extraordinary Old Town has a large main square and many churches and palaces. Wawel Castle, which was once the seat of the government, looks down from a cliff high above the Vistula River.

Lodz is Poland's third-largest city, with a population of nearly 740,000. It is located in central Poland, less than 100 miles (160 km) southwest of the capital city of Warsaw. Lodz was a small town until the 1800s, when it became a center for textile manufacturing. During the devastation of World War II, Lodz's population dropped by

more than half, including about three hundred thousand Jewish residents. Today, Lodz remains a major industrial center with a large textile industry. It is also an important educational center. The Museum of Art in Lodz has an excellent collection of European modern art.

Wroclaw, with a population of about 630,000, is Poland's fourth-largest city. It is located in southwestern Poland. As national borders have been redrawn over the years, it has at times been part of nearby countries, including Germany, Austria, Bohemia, and Prussia. Remnants of these cultures are still evident in Wroclaw today. Wroclaw lies along the Oder River, and has sometimes suffered devastating flooding. One of the worst floods occurred in July 1997, when nearly one-third of the city was underwater. Wroclaw is a center for cultural and artistic activity. It is the site of a large jazz festival and was the home of the experimental Polish Laboratory Theater. Many visitors enjoy strolling through the historic Market Square, which is lined with brightly colored buildings (above).

Poznan, Poland's fifth-largest city, home to about 550,000 people, lies in the west-central part of the country. It has a colorful history. It was a major political center in early Poland and served as the capital throughout most of the 1200s. Today, it is a center of trade, sports, education, and technology. Poznan's cathedral dates to the tenth century and is one of the oldest churches in Poland.

Rain falls all year long, with an average annual total of about 24 inches (60 cm). Rainfall is heaviest in the summer and lightest in the winter, and it rains more frequently in the mountain areas than in the lowlands.

Protecting the Environment

In the twentieth century, Poland became one of the most polluted countries in the world. Waste from industry fouled the waters and burning coal sent pollutants into the air. The air pollution produced acid rain, which damaged trees and dirtied

Light rain is common throughout the year in Warsaw.

lakes. It also caused breathing difficulties and other health problems for the population. Water from many rivers was so dirty that it could not be used to water crops.

In the 1980s, Poland began an effort to reduce the pollution. Some of the most polluting industrial plants were shut down. Since then, technology has improved, so that factories, power plants, and cars don't produce as much pollution. Limits

The Dunajec River runs through southern Poland, past the dramatic Pieniny Mountains.

have also been placed on the amount of pollutants allowed into the air and water. These changes have helped tremendously, and Poland is on the road to having a cleaner environment.

The government has also set aside many areas of land as national parks or preserves to help protect regions of great beauty or habitats that are vital to plants or animals. For example, Table Mountains National Park protects an area of unusual sandstone formations. Karkonosze National Park includes some of Poland's most beautiful mountains. The nation's largest national park is Biebrza, which protects a marshy area around the Biebrza River in northeastern Poland. Biebrza National Park is a crucial stopping point for migrating birds. The park also contains many rare plants, including twenty species of orchids.

Karkonosze National Park is renowned for its varied landscapes, which include lakes, bogs, and fantastic rock formations.

CHAPTER 3

All Creatures Great and Small

POLAND IS HOME TO THOUSANDS OF ANIMAL SPECIES. Some live in the country year-round, while others stop in for a time before moving on. Birds are among the most common visitors. Poland regularly hosts more than two hundred bird species, with another two hundred having been spotted at one time or another. Poland also has nearly a hundred mammal species and about fifty varieties of fish.

Birds

Poland has a wealth of bird life. It is a critical breeding ground for many migratory species, which travel to the region solely to reproduce. In fact, Poland hosts about a quarter of all the migratory species on the European continent. Poland's wetlands in the lake region and along the Baltic provide the birds with an ideal environment. Many of these habitats are protected by Polish law.

Opposite: **Red deer are one of the largest deer species. They are common in Poland.**

A green sandpiper bathes in the Biebrza region. These birds spend much of their time in shallow water, picking insects and other food from the mud.

The Biebrza marshes in northeastern Poland make up a vital wetland region that serves as a habitat for many of Poland's endangered bird species, from rare owls and sandpipers to terns, snipes, and some eagle varieties. Poland also has what is believed to be the largest population of aquatic warblers in the world. These small brown songbirds are one of the most endangered birds in Europe.

For the Birds

The Polish Society for the Protection of Birds was launched in 1991 with the purpose of protecting Poland's many bird species and the habitats where they live. Today, it is one of the largest conservation groups in the country, with more than two thousand members and a full-time staff. The society focuses its attention on the most pressing threats, such as habitat destruction or diminishing numbers of the rarest species, as well as on fund-raising campaigns and public awareness programs. One of the society's most notable recent projects has been managing the habitat of the aquatic warbler (left), a threatened species. It has also worked to protect marshlands, forests, and many other areas.

Many Mammals

Many kinds of mammals make their home in Poland. Among the smallest are wild hamsters, which live near farmlands along with other tiny, furry beasts such as mice and voles. Poland also has several species of rabbits, squirrels, marmots, and hedgehogs. Predators in Poland include foxes, lynx, and wildcats. Deer and elk roam forests, and the Tatra Mountains are home to the chamois, a beautiful goatlike creature. The Tatras also are a habitat for brown bears. A large herd of European bison lives in Bialowieza Forest, on the Poland-Belarus border.

Sea Life

Poland is rich in rivers and lakes, so it is not surprising that it also hosts an impressive variety of fish. Some of the most abundant fish varieties include perch, pike, bream, carp,

Grand Bird

The white-tailed eagle is a large bird of prey found across many parts of Europe and northern Asia. Some people believe it is the inspiration for the white eagle shown on the Polish coat of arms. The white eagle grows up to 3 feet (1 m) long from beak to tail and boasts a wingspan of nearly 8 feet (2.4 m). It is a magnificent animal in appearance, with feathers of varying brown shades often tipped with white or cream, a yellowish beak and claws, and a flash of bright white on the tail. Since the 1800s, the species has suffered a dramatic decline in population, mostly because of pollution and overhunting by people who mistakenly considered it a threat to livestock. Conservation efforts began in the 1980s, and today, the numbers of white-tailed eagles is rising.

bleak, and roach. Bleak and roach are found throughout the country, favoring all but the most rapidly moving waterways.

Pike are one of the many kinds of fish that swim in Polish waters. They are a large species, often growing 2 to 4 feet (0.6 to 1.2 m) long.

Trout and salmon come to Poland's rivers to spawn, or reproduce, and Polish law protects many of their favored areas. Herring and cod thrive in the Baltic Sea, as do some types of shellfish and jellyfish.

Reptiles and Amphibians

Only nine kinds of reptiles live in Poland. Four species of snakes and four species of lizards can be found in the country. The only

Bringing Back the Bison

European bison are the heaviest land animal in Europe. The massive creatures grow 7 to 10 feet (2 to 3 m) long and weigh between 500 and 2,000 pounds (220 to 900 kilograms).

There was a time when thousands of European bison roamed the Polish landscape. But the animals were prized for their meat and hides, and their horns were often used as drinking vessels. By the early 1900s, they were hunted nearly to extinction. In the late 1920s, only about fifty European bison existed, and they were all in zoos and preserves.

Beginning in the 1930s, however, a group of Polish scientists began a breeding program. Bison were released into the wild again in the early 1950s. By the 1970s their numbers had grown to the hundreds, and today there are many stable populations. About eight hundred bison live in the Bialowieza Forest. This is the largest herd anywhere. The bison is still considered a threatened species, but thanks to conservationists, it has been spared the fate of extinction.

A Visit to the Krakow Zoo

The Krakow Zoo is one of Poland's oldest zoos still in operation. It opened in 1929 and is located in a wooded area known as Park Miejski. The zoo boasts a collection of some 1,500 animals representing more than 250 species. Some of the most interesting include a herd of pygmy hippopotamuses, which are nearly extinct in the wild, and a herd of Przewalski's horses, which at one time were extinct in the wild but have since been reintroduced in very small numbers. The zoo has taken part in many notable breeding programs, successfully reproducing rare species such as the Andean condor, the white-handed gibbon, and the snow leopard.

turtle native to Poland is the European pond turtle, which lives near wetlands and grows 5 to 15 inches (13 to 38 cm) long.

Amphibians found in Poland include newts, toads, and several species of frogs. These include the tree frog, the laughing frog, and the common frog.

Snake in the Grass

One of the most common snakes in Europe is the grass snake. It is usually found near water—and since Poland has so much of that, the grass snake is fairly abundant there. It feeds primarily on amphibians such as frogs, toads, and salamanders, but will also eat fish, worms, and a few insects. Grass snakes generally grow about 3 to 4 feet (1 to 1.2 m) long. When threatened by predators, they sometimes flip onto their backs and play dead. Their predators include foxes, cats, a variety of birds, and humans.

Trees and Plants

At one time, most of Poland was forested. Over the centuries, however, much of these forests were cut down, so that today, only a little more than one-quarter of Poland is forested. The largest stretch of continuous forest today is the Lower Silesian Wilderness in southwestern Poland.

In recent years, forests have been replanted, although the types of trees that make up the forests have changed. Many deciduous tree species—those that lose their leaves in the winter—have been replaced with evergreen trees such as pines. So many evergreens have been planted that pines and spruces now make up the great bulk of trees found in Polish forests. They are hardy in temperate weather and support undergrowth such as berry bushes and a variety of lichens and mosses. Polish forests also still include common oak, common elm, black alder, and white willow.

Deciduous trees turn a beautiful shade of gold in a forest in northeastern Poland.

A variety of larch tree called the Polish larch is found exclusively in the lowland regions of northern Poland. Poland is also host to a rare variety of chrysanthemum that looks similar to the white-and-yellow daisies commonly found in the United States.

In the spring, wildflowers brighten the nation's meadows. Common flowers include crocuses, flax, and corn poppies. The bright red corn poppy is an unofficial symbol of Poland.

Red poppies bloom in late spring, bringing a burst of color to Polish fields.

The Ancient Forest

Stepping into Bialowieza Forest is like going back in time. Lying on the border between Poland and Belarus, it is one of the few remaining parts of a forest that once covered much of the European lowlands. Oak, lime, spruce, and alder grow tall and slender in this forest. One section of the Bialowieza Forest is a primeval forest, which means that it has been growing relatively undisturbed for centuries. It was never logged. Logging, hunting, and wood collecting are allowed in other parts of the forest.

The primeval Bialowieza Forest has the tallest trees in Europe, but it also has abundant fallen trees, which is vital to having a healthy ecosystem. Thousands of species of insects eat the dead trees, and birds and other creatures eat the insects. It is estimated that half of the

forest's twelve thousand species rely on the decaying trees on the forest floor for survival. The forest is home to the world's largest herd of European bison, as well as moose, bear, lynx, wolves, foxes, beavers, owls, eagles, and eight species of woodpecker.

The forest was spared human interference centuries ago when Polish kings declared it off-limits to other people so it could be used as a royal hunting ground. The Polish government protected the oldest section as a national park in the early 1920s. Today, many environmentalists want to expand the protected area, but many local people work as foresters cutting trees. Many others rely on wood from the forest to heat their homes. They argue that they use the forest responsibly and there is no reason to protect it more. The arguments continue, but everyone agrees that they are living near one of the most extraordinary places in the country.

CHAPTER 4

Past and Present

THE EARLIEST EVIDENCE OF HUMANS IN THE AREA now called Poland dates back about one hundred thousand years. Neanderthals, early relatives of modern humans, likely hunted in the southern region of the country. Early *Homo sapiens*—the modern human species—began building settlements somewhere around 8000 to 6000 BCE. Beginning in about 600 BCE, these early Polish communities were sometimes invaded by other Eurasian groups, including early Celts and Germans.

Opposite: **Neanderthals lived across much of Europe and Asia. They lived in small groups and used tools to hunt animals.**

Early Times

In the sixth century CE, various Slavonic tribes arrived in the region. Where exactly the Slavs originated is still the subject of debate, but they spread to many parts of Europe and Asia. The Slavs were already relatively advanced technologically and socially when they arrived in the region of Poland, and it did not take long for them to become the most influential group in the area. They established tribal government, trade routes, and defensive forces. Within the Slavonic ranks, the Polan tribe became dominant by the tenth century. Poland's name came from this group.

The reign of Mieszko I lasted about thirty years. During that time, he vastly expanded Polish lands.

The Piastian Kings

In 966, a Polanian prince named Mieszko I was baptized, and many people consider this the year that Poland became Christian. Mieszko was regarded as a descendant of Piast the Wheelwright, a legendary figure in Polish history, and thus he and his heirs formed what became known as the Piast dynasty.

Mieszko and his son Boleslaw I oversaw the continuing development of Poland both at home and abroad. They expanded the nation by taking over surrounding lands, often through sheer military might. They also formed a centralized government and increased Poland's involvement in European affairs. By the time of Mieszko's death, in 992, Poland stretched from the Baltic Sea to the Carpathian Mountains, as it does today.

Casimir I reunited parts of Poland that had been lost during wars with neighboring nations. The Catholic Church also became stronger during his reign.

During the reign of Mieszko's grandson, Mieszko II, Poland suffered through civil war and attacks from neighboring countries. As a result, Poland lost some of its territory and the government became unstable.

Some stability returned with the reigns of Mieszko II's son Casimir, and Casimir's son Boleslaw II. But by the time Boleslaw's nephew took the throne in the early 1100s, the country was once again mired in conflict, and Poland lost much of its international standing as a result. It would be more than two hundred years before the nation regained its status in Europe. Nevertheless, Poland underwent some notable

Medieval Poland

- Poland under Mieszko I, ca. 990
- Poland under Boleslaw I, 992–1018
- Present-day boundary

advancements during this period, including the founding of thousands of new settlements and the establishment of many monasteries.

The late 1300s saw an increase in Polish influence in Europe. Krakow became an important political center as well as the home to Poland's first major university. The University of Krakow educated Poland's greatest thinkers.

During this period, Poland also attracted large numbers of migrants. Many Germans moved east into Poland. The Jewish community in Poland was also growing and thriving during this time. In many parts of Europe, Jewish people were treated badly and sometimes were forced to become Christian. But in Poland, the leaders tended to protect the Jewish population.

The Jagiellon Dynasty

In 1386, Queen Jadwiga of Poland married Jagiello, the Grand Duke of Lithuania. This united the two countries and launched what would become known as the Jagiellon dynasty. The Jagiellon rulers oversaw a period of relative prosperity and growth for both Poland and Lithuania. During this period, Polish and Lithuanian forces battled the Teutonic Knights, a Germanic group that was fighting for control near the Baltic.

In 1410, the Poles and Lithuanians were victorious at the Battle of Tannenberg, in what is now northeastern Poland. Poland also successfully defended against the Ottoman Empire and the Crimean Tatars in the southern region of the country. Additionally, the Poles aided Lithuania in its battles against the forces led by the Grand Duchy of Moscow.

Sigismund II Augustus was the last Jagiellon ruler. By his reign, Poland had expanded into Ukraine and Russia. He also oversaw a flourishing of the Polish economy and culture. During this time, Polish astronomer Nicolaus Copernicus made the groundbreaking discovery that the earth is not the center of the universe, but instead orbits the sun.

Polish and Lithuanian forces won a major victory at the Battle of Tannenberg. They killed or captured most of the leaders of the Teutonic Knights.

Studying the Sky

In 1473, a boy named Nicolaus Copernicus was born in Torun, a city in northern Poland. He would grow up to become the founder of modern astronomy.

Copernicus came from a wealthy family. At about age eighteen, he moved to Krakow, where he attended the University of Krakow and delved into mathematics and astronomy. In the coming years, Copernicus would spend a great deal of time studying the sky.

At the time, the dominant theory in astronomy was that the earth sat still at the center of the universe. According to this idea, all the other planets and stars moved around the earth. But as Copernicus studied the planets, their movement did not seem to follow this idea.

They were not orbiting the earth. In the early 1500s, Copernicus came up with the idea that the earth was one of several planets that orbited the sun. The idea was revolutionary.

Copernicus was so concerned that people would object to his theory that he refused to publish his book *On the Revolutions of Heavenly Spheres*, which contained his observations and ideas. The book did not appear until 1543, shortly before Copernicus died. It had a major impact, however, greatly influencing scientists such as Galileo Galilei and Johannes Kepler, who would soon radically change the way humankind understood the universe.

The Polish-Lithuanian Commonwealth

In 1569, an agreement called the Union of Lublin formally established the Polish-Lithuanian Commonwealth. By 1573, the monarchs who led the commonwealth were elected, rather than inheriting the title from family members. The commonwealth was one of the most influential nations in all of Europe, and had a strong military. Commonwealth troops engaged in battles with Russia, the Ottoman Empire, and Sweden. They also controlled attacks by the Cossacks, a people who hailed from Russia and Ukraine.

Polish troops are forced from Moscow, Russia, in 1612. Sigismund III, the leader of the Polish-Lithuanian Commonwealth, tried but failed to gain control of Russia.

Warfare weakened the commonwealth in the mid-seventeenth century. As a result, the population dwindled, the economy and infrastructure were damaged, and the nation's leaders faced a period of turmoil. By the mid-eighteenth century, the population and economy were growing again, but the commonwealth never fully regained its position on the world stage.

Partition

In 1772, the three powers surrounding the Polish-Lithuanian Commonwealth—Russia, Austria, and the German kingdom of Prussia—began chipping away at the commonwealth. They each annexed, or portioned, part of it. In 1793, each of the powers annexed more of the commonwealth, leaving only a small part independent. In 1794, General Tadeusz Kosciuszko, a Polish officer who had fought in the American Revolution, raised an army of peasants to try to force out Poland's conquerors. They were defeated, however, and Kosciuszko was captured. With a third partition in 1795, the commonwealth, and Poland, disappeared from the map.

Although Poland was not an independent nation during its partitioned era, the culture and identity

Polish-Lithuanian Commonwealth

Lands lost 1657–1686   Present-day boundary

Kosciuszko Mound

In Krakow, there stands an interesting sight—a large cone-shaped mound covered in green grass. A path spiraling to the top looks, from a distance, like a winding white stripe. And at the very peak, more than 1,070 feet (326 m) above sea level, stands a simple cross. This is the Kosciuszko Mound, built in the early 1800s to honor Polish leader Tadeusz Kosciuszko.

Kosciuszko, who was born in 1746, grew up to become one of Poland's greatest heroes. He led two revolutionary battles in the quest for freedom against Russia after having traveled to America to fight against the British during the American Revolution. He was a lifelong believer in the personal rights of humans. One of his best friends, U.S. president Thomas Jefferson, admired him greatly.

Kosciuszko died in Switzerland in 1817, and construction on the mound bearing his name began shortly thereafter. Kosciuszko Mound remains a popular monument, with thousands of people making the long walk to the top every year.

that had formed during the previous centuries could not be diminished. They were kept alive in the hearts of Polish people who resented the loss of freedom. Thus, the partitioned era was characterized by countless rebellions as Poles tried to rid themselves of their conquerors.

One of the most notable rebellions was the November Uprising. It began in late November 1830 and lasted about seven months. During that time, Polish rebels drove Russian

Partitions of Poland

RUSSIA

PRUSSIA

PRUSSIA

AUSTRIA

OTTOMAN EMPIRE

—— Boundaries in 1772

—— Present-day Poland

First Partition, 1772

  to Austria

  to Prussia

  to Russia

Second Partition, 1793

  to Prussia

  to Russia

Third Partition, 1795

  to Austria

  to Prussia

  to Russia

forces out of Warsaw, and, for a time, prevented the Russians from regaining control of the city. Nevertheless, the uprising was ultimately defeated, because the rebels did not receive the international support that they needed to maintain their military supplies. Another uprising in 1863, known as the January Uprising, met a similar fate.

Independent Again

Poland underwent tremendous changes in the first half of the twentieth century. Millions of Polish troops took part in World War I, and nearly half a million lost their lives. When the war was over, Poland won its independence once again.

Jozef Pilsudski, a man known as the Founder of Modern Poland, was named Poland's head of state and the commander in chief of its army. He had been a military leader during World War I. Pilsudski was in charge of creating a new national government, and he oversaw the writing of a new Polish constitution.

Poland continued to experience turmoil during these years. Polish forces battled Russians in what is called the Polish-Soviet War. The Poles decisively defeated the Russians

Scientific Superstar

Marie Curie is one of the greatest scientists ever to come out of Poland. Born Marie Sklodowska in Warsaw in 1867, she showed extraordinary scientific talent from an early age. She moved to Paris in 1891 to attend university. She soon earned a degree in physics and then a second degree in mathematical sciences.

In 1903, she won the Nobel Prize in Physics (along with her husband, Pierre Curie, and another scientist named Henri Becquerel) for the groundbreaking discovery of radioactivity. In 1911, she won the Nobel Prize in Chemistry on her own, for the discovery of two elements—radium and polonium. She named the latter in honor of her home country. She was the first woman to win the Nobel Prize and the only person to win the Nobel Prize in two different sciences.

Curie also founded two major scientific institutes—one in Paris and the other in Warsaw—that continue to operate to this day. She died in 1934.

in 1920. Poland gained land to the east that was home to many Ukrainians and Belarusians.

The country was not stable, however. Pilsudski stepped aside as head of state when national elections were held in 1922. The newly elected president Gabriel Narutowicz was soon assassinated. The government continued to be chaotic. Finally, in 1926, Pilsudski led a coup that enabled him to take control of Poland. He soon established a dictatorship. When he died in 1935, however, there was no obvious person to assume power. This made the nation once again weak and vulnerable. Poland's independence would be short-lived.

Adolf Hitler salutes German troops as they march through Warsaw in 1939. About 1.5 million German soldiers took part in the invasion of Poland.

World War II

In the 1930s, Germany began demanding that Poland turn over control of the city of Gdansk, which it considered German territory. In August 1939, Germany and the Soviet Union signed a nonaggression pact, agreeing not to attack each other. A few days later, Germany invaded Poland, beginning World War II. England and France both supported Poland and declared war on Germany. A few weeks later, Soviet forces moved into eastern Poland. The nation was once again under the control of foreign nations, with Germany controlling one half and the Soviet Union controlling the other half.

World War II devastated Poland and its people. Early in the war, the Soviet Union deported more than one million people in eastern Poland to the Soviet Union. Meanwhile, the Germans herded the country's Jewish population—the largest in Europe, at about three million—into controlled neighborhoods called ghettos. Later, they were sent to death camps, where they were murdered. Five hundred thousand Jews lived in a tiny area that was the Warsaw Ghetto. Hunger and disease killed thousands. Beginning in 1942, five thousand people a day were taken from the ghetto and shipped to a death camp. In 1943, the people in the Warsaw Ghetto staged an uprising, pre-

The Auschwitz-Birkenau State Museum

The unimaginable hardships endured by the Polish people during World War II can still be felt in one of the nation's

most moving landmarks—the Auschwitz-Birkenau State Museum. Located in southern Poland, it sits on the site of two notorious Nazi camps: Auschwitz I and Auschwitz II-Birkenau. Auschwitz I was a concentration camp, where people were forced to work, often to death. Auschwitz II-Birkenau was a death camp where people were killed with poisonous gas. More than a million people died at the camps. About 90 percent of them were Jewish, while the remainder were ethnic Poles, Roma (Gypsies), and people of other diverse nationalities.

The camp has been preserved to look much as it did during the war. More than a million people visit every year. As they enter, they pass through a gate beneath a large metal sign that reads *Arbeit macht frei*, German for "work makes you free." They then make their way around the eerily silent buildings and fields, remembering.

venting deportations to the death camps for several weeks. But in the end, the uprising was brutally crushed. By the end of the war, the Nazi regime had killed almost all the Jews in Poland.

In 1941, Germany attacked the Soviet Union, so the Soviets entered the war on the side of the Allies—England, France, and eventually the United States. After this, a Polish army was created to fight in the war. Many Poles were also underground fighters who resisted Germany secretly, rather than being part of a formal army. In 1944, Polish resistance fighters staged a major uprising in Warsaw to try to force the Germans from the city.

German troops round up the surviving Jews after the destruction of the Warsaw Ghetto in 1943.

During the uprising and its aftermath, German forces destroyed more than half the buildings in Warsaw.

By the war's end, more than six million people had been killed in Poland. Warsaw and other cities had been reduced to rubble, and the land was devastated.

After the War

The end of the war did not free Poland from Soviet influence. The Soviet Union retained control of areas it had gained in 1939. Many Poles from eastern, Soviet-occupied regions were resettled in western Poland, from which Germans had been expelled. A communist government was set up in Poland, and the Soviets held power over this government. The Polish government nationalized industry and took over a great deal of land. Unlike in many other communist countries, however, the church remained powerful in Poland.

In 1956, Wladyslaw Gomulka became the leader of the communist party in Poland, the most powerful position in Poland at the time. Gomulka was somewhat less restrictive than previous leaders. He released some political prisoners

Poland in World War II

—— Boundaries in 1939	→ German invasion Sep. 1–Oct. 6, 1939
—— Present-day Poland	← Soviet invasion Sep. 17–Oct. 6, 1939
⚝ Battle	▢ Occupied by Germany
▢ Concentration camp	▢ Occupied by the Soviet Union

Solidarity leader Lech Walesa speaks to striking workers in 1980. Solidarity was the first labor union independent of communist control in a country under Soviet influence.

from jail and allowed more personal freedom. These changes did not last, however, and groups opposing the communist government continued to be persecuted.

Independence at Last

In the 1970s, food prices were rising quickly, and riots erupted in several cities. At the same time, workers began demanding the right to form their own trade unions. Lech Walesa, an electrician at the Gdansk shipyards, led workers on a strike.

Soon, several unions were working together as part of a group called Solidarity. This group evolved into a powerful political entity working for greater freedom. The government tried to crush Solidarity, but it continued to be a powerful force.

Throughout the 1980s, the power of the communist government began to erode. In 1989, Solidarity's Tadeusz Mazowiecki was elected prime minister. He was the first noncommunist to be prime minister of Poland since World War II.

Then, in 1990, the Polish people elected Lech Walesa president. This victory marked not only a turning point in Poland's efforts to regain its independence but also the beginning of the end of Soviet power throughout Europe. The Soviet Union itself dissolved in 1991, becoming fifteen separate nations—the largest and most powerful being Russia.

Lech Walesa

Lech Walesa is one of the most important figures in modern Polish history. He was born in 1943 in Popowo, a town in north-central Poland. His father was arrested and put in a concentration camp by the Germans before Lech was born. Walesa's father managed to return home after the war ended but died shortly thereafter. This had a deep effect on Walesa, who learned to be tough in the face of opposition.

Walesa became an electrician. In the 1970s, he grew frustrated with the oppression by the communist government and organized his fellow workers into a resistance group called Solidarity. By the 1980s, the Solidarity movement was growing in power. As the Soviet Union crumbled and lost control of Poland, Poles elected Walesa president. He spent much of his presidency helping the country make the transition from communism to capitalism. He is still active in Polish politics today and often lectures about the importance of national freedom.

In the 1990s, Poland transformed itself from a communist to a capitalist society, and its economy grew at a remarkable pace. Poland joined the European Union (EU) in 2004. The EU is a union of nations that form a common market so that goods can pass freely among the member countries without being taxed.

In recent years, Poland has flourished as a modern, democratic nation. It has experienced tremendous turmoil and change in the last century, but today it is one of the most powerful nations in Europe.

Crowds fill the town square in Wroclaw to celebrate Poland joining the European Union.

A National Tragedy

On April 10, 2010, tragedy struck the nation of Poland when a Polish Air Force jet crashed just outside the Russian city of Smolensk, killing all ninety-six people on board. Among those passengers were some of the most important people in Poland, including the president, Lech Kaczynski, and his wife, Maria (photo right); former president Ryszard Kaczorowski; fifteen members of Poland's parliament; and several high-ranking members of the Catholic Church in Poland.

Because the accident occurred in Russia, Russian authorities launched an investigation. Polish authorities also began an investigation. They did this, in part, because Poland and Russia have such a long, tense history and some members of the public were suspicious that the Russian government somehow might have been involved in the crash. In the end, however, both the Poles and the Russians determined that the cause of the accident was pilot error.

CHAPTER 5

The Halls of Government

THE NATION OF POLAND IS KNOWN FORMALLY AS THE Republic of Poland. A republic is a nation in which power ultimately lies with the people because they choose their leaders in elections. Polish citizens have been enjoying this privilege for a generation now. Like the United States, Poland's government has three branches—executive, legislative, and judicial.

Opposite: **Bronislaw Komorowski became president of Poland in 2010.**

Executive Branch

The executive branch is the part of government that executes, or carries out, laws. It also oversees the military, proposes and carries out policies, and performs general administrative duties. In Poland, the head of the executive branch is the president. But Poland's executive branch differs from that of the United States in that it also has a prime minister. The president is Poland's head of state, while the prime minister is the head of the government.

National Government of Poland

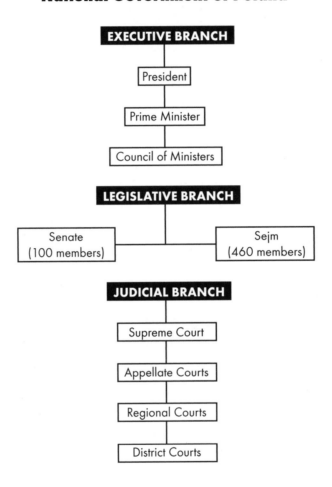

The president acts as the representative of the nation, performing symbolic duties, but has only limited political power. The president's powers include commanding military forces and being able to veto any laws passed by the parliament, the nation's lawmaking body. The president is elected to a five-year term and can serve two terms. Bronislaw Komorowski was elected in 2010.

The prime minister, on the other hand, oversees the day-to-day affairs of parliament, while presiding over the Council of Ministers, or the cabinet. The members of the cabinet oversee various departments, such as foreign affairs, education, and the environment. The prime minister is assisted by the deputy prime minister.

The prime minister is the leader of the political party that won the most seats in parliament in the previous election. If no one party won a majority of seats, then two or more parties join together in a coalition and choose a leader. Donald Tusk, the leader of the Civic Platform Party, became prime minister in 2007.

As prime minister since 2007, Donald Tusk has worked for greater integration between Poland and the rest of Europe.

Legislative Branch

The legislative branch of the Polish government is its parliament. Like the U.S. Congress, it has two parts. The Senate has 100 members, and the Sejm has 460 members. All are elected to four-year terms. All citizens at least eighteen years old may vote.

For a bill to become a law, both the Senate and the Sejm must approve it. The Sejm also approves members of the cabinet.

The Polish Parliament listens to a speech by French president François Hollande in 2012.

Judicial Branch

The role of the judicial branch is to ensure that laws are interpreted and applied fairly. The highest court in Poland

is the Supreme Court. The Supreme Court supervises lower courts. It also hears appeals of cases handled in lower courts. The National Judicial Council nominates the Supreme Court judges and the president appoints them to a term for life. The president also appoints the head of the Supreme Court, called the first president of the Supreme Court, to a six-year term.

District and provincial courts handle criminal and civil cases as well as labor and family matters. Appellate courts review decisions made in lower courts. Special military courts handle criminal matters relating to the Polish armed services, and Poland's administrative courts handle legal matters where various administrative bodies are concerned, including corporations and other organizations.

The Polish Supreme Court meets in a modern building in Warsaw.

Exploring the Capital

Warsaw is Poland's capital as well as its largest city, with more than 1.7 million residents. In the Polish language, Warsaw is known as Warszawa, which means "property of Warsz" and probably refers to a twelfth-century man named Warsz who owned land in the neighborhood that is now called Mariensztat.

The city is located in the east-central part of the country. It is one of Poland's oldest communities, with the first settlements established in the Brodno neighborhood in the late 800s. Over the centuries, Warsaw has been subject to many wartime attacks. During World War II, almost 90 percent of the buildings in the city were reduced to rubble. After the war, the city came back to life. Many large apartment buildings were constructed to house all the people who had lost their homes. Some of the historic parts of Warsaw were carefully rebuilt.

Today, Warsaw is a vibrant city, with a robust business center, museums and art galleries, universities, and sports stadiums. The city also has extensive parklands. A full quarter of the city land is devoted to parks, nature reserves, and other green spaces. As the seat of the Polish government, Warsaw is home to the national parliament, the Supreme Court, and the president's offices.

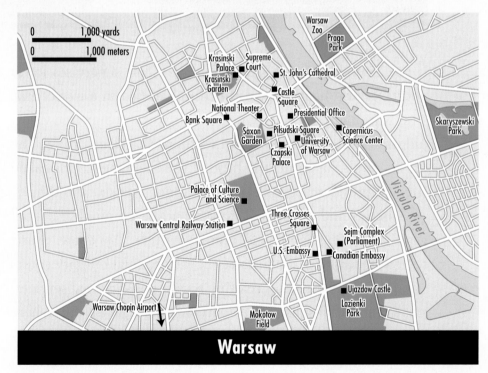

Warsaw

Another important part of Poland's judiciary is the Constitutional Tribunal. The tribunal's function is to ensure that all parts of Poland's constitution are honored. It is a fully independent body consisting of fifteen judges who are appointed by the Sejm and serve nine-year terms. They review the activities of the government, proposed laws, actions of political parties, and some international issues.

A second independent group, the State Tribunal, acts as a watchdog group to ensure the legality of government activities. If someone is accused of violating the constitution, the state tribunal will review the case. It has the ability to remove

Justices on the Constitutional Tribunal may serve only one term.

A child helps her father vote at a polling station in Warsaw.

people from power, block appointments, prevent people from running for office, and even remove titles and honors. The State Tribunal consists of nineteen members, including the first president of the Supreme Court.

Poland's Flag

The Polish flag was adopted in 1919. It consists of two horizontal bars: the top one white and the bottom one red. White and red have been the traditional national colors of Poland since the thirteenth century, although they were not named the country's official national colors until 1831.

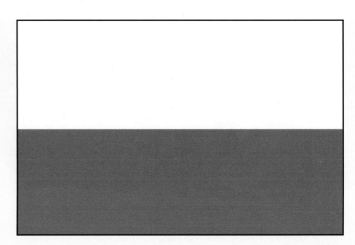

Political Parties

Poland has two main political parties—the Civic Platform Party and the Law and Justice Party. The Civic Platform Party was founded in 2001. It is a politically centrist party that generally supports integration with the rest of Europe and tends to be conservative on social issues. It has held power since the elections of 2007, and its members include Poland's current president, Bronislaw Komorowski; the prime minister, Donald

Jaroslaw Kaczynski, the leader of the Law and Justice Party, was first elected to parliament in 1991.

Voivodeships

Tusk; plus majorities in both the Sejm and the Senate. The Law and Justice Party was also founded in 2001 and is more conservative than the Civic Platform Party. Its chairman and cofounder, Jaroslaw Kaczynski, the identical twin brother of former president Lech Kaczynski, served as prime minister from 2006 to 2007.

Other political parties active in Poland include the Polish People's Party, which represents farmers and other working-class citizens; the Democratic Left Alliance, which takes a more liberal stance on most issues; the United Poland Party, which reflects a conservative stance often parallel to the Catholic Church; and Palikot's Movement, an extremely liberal party that opposes the influence of religious clergy on the government.

Regional Government

Poland is divided into sections called *voivodeships*, which are similar to U.S. states. These are further divided into *powiats* (counties) and *gminas* (towns and cities). At present there are sixteen voivodeships, nearly four hundred powiats, and more than 2,400 gminas.

Poland's National Anthem

The national anthem of Poland is "Mazurek Dabrowskiego" ("Poland Is Not Yet Lost"). The lyrics were written by Polish general Jozef Rufin Wybicki in 1797, just two years after the partitions ended the Polish-Lithuanian Commonwealth, wiping Poland off the map. The music is a folk tune.

Polish lyrics

Jeszcze Polska nie zginela,
Kiedy my zyjemy.
Co nam obca przemoc wziela,
Szabla odbierzemy.

Marsz, marsz, Dabrowski,
Z ziemi wloskiej do Polski.
Za twoim przewodem
Zlaczym sie z narodem.

Przejdziem Wisle, przejdziem Warte,
Bedziem Polakami.
Dal nam przyklad Bonaparte,
Jak zwyciezac mamy.

Marsz, marsz, Dabrowski,
Z ziemi wloskiej do Polski.
Za twoim przewodem
Zlaczym sie z narodem.

English translation

Poland has not yet perished,
So long as we still live.
What the alien force has taken from us,
We shall retrieve with a saber.

March, march, Dabrowski,
From the Italian land to Poland.
Under your command
We shall rejoin the nation.

We'll cross the Vistula and the Warta,
We shall be Polish.
Bonaparte has given us the example
Of how we should prevail.

March, march, Dabrowski,
From the Italian land to Poland.
Under your command
We shall rejoin the nation.

CHAPTER 6

A New Economy

I N 1989, AS COMMUNIST RULE ENDED IN POLAND, the nation's economy was in terrible shape. The country faced crushing foreign debt, rising unemployment, and runaway inflation. At one point, prices were going up more than 600 percent a year. The Polish government tried to fix these problems, but the solutions proved ineffective. It became obvious that more drastic measures were required.

Shock Therapy

Minister of Finance Leszek Balcerowicz came up with a series of radical reforms. These reforms are known as shock therapy because they consist of major abrupt changes. The plan included an increase in imports, wage controls, and a sweeping transition from government-controlled businesses to privatized businesses. These changes encouraged competitiveness and, as a result, produced better products and services. To help private businesses get started, Poland also made changes to its banking system, offering more opportunity to borrow money. Additional aid came from

Clerks ring up purchases at a large grocery store in Wroclaw. About 64 percent of Poles work in services such as retail sales.

foreign governments who kept cash reserves on hand to help the Polish government make the necessary changes.

As a result of these reforms, Poland's economy improved rapidly. At first, however, there were some problems. Unemployment and inflation were high. But by 1992, tens of thousands of new companies had been launched, more than a million new jobs had been created, inflation had dropped to less than 50 percent for the first time in years, the country's international debt was cut in half, and foreign investors began looking to Poland for new opportunities. The gross domestic product (GDP), the total value of goods and services produced by a nation in one year, grew significantly. By the following year, inflation dropped to less than 10 percent, and Poland was on its way to having a stable economy.

The Economy Today

Today, Poland has one of the strongest economies in Europe. In fact, it was the only country in the European Union with an economy that did not shrink during the global financial crisis that began in 2008. The Polish economy has an annual

Businesspeople talk in the lobby of an office building in Warsaw. About 8 percent of Polish people work in finance or real estate.

growth rate of about 3 percent, which places it well above most other countries. In 2013, the inflation rate was about 4 percent. Unemployment, however, remains high. About 12 percent of the people in Poland who are looking for work cannot find jobs.

Service Industries

Service industries account for more than 60 percent of the Polish GDP. Services are when someone does something for someone else rather than making, growing, or mining a product. Mowing lawns and answering telephones are services. Doctors, teachers, bus drivers, store clerks, bankers, and

Success Story

Leszek Czarnecki is one of Poland's most successful business leaders. Born in Wroclaw in 1962, he studied environmental engineering at Wroclaw University of Technology before receiving a PhD from Wroclaw University of Economics. He was the chief executive officer (CEO) of Polbank S.A. in the mid-1990s and then became CEO of the insurance company Europa S.A. In the mid-2000s he moved to Getin, financial company. Under his guidance, Getin began acquiring interest in many international businesses, including some in Russia, Belarus, and Ukraine. The *Wall Street Journal* has called Czarnecki the best CEO in central Europe. In 2009, Ernst & Young, a company that does accounting and provides other services, dubbed him Entrepreneur of the Year. He has written several books, including *Simply Business*, which explains how to become a successful entrepreneur.

auto mechanics all work in services. Poland's service sector has become particularly attractive to businesses from other nations that hire Polish firms for such jobs as accounting, research and development, and software design. The United States is Poland's biggest international customer. American companies employ about one-third of the Poles who work in services. Other leading customer nations include France and Germany. Most business experts predict that the tremendous growth in this area will continue, which encourages more Polish citizens to seek higher education.

Workers assemble cars at a factory in southern Poland. The vast majority of cars built in Poland are exported to other countries to be sold.

Manufacturing

The second-largest slice of Poland's economy is industry, which makes up about one-third of the GDP. Industry

Necklaces made of amber beads hang in a market in Gdansk. Poland is one of the world's largest producers of amber.

includes construction and the manufacture of everything from food products to airplanes. Poland's leading products include ships, machinery, automobiles, furniture, food and beverage items, glass, paper, and textiles.

Mining and Energy

Mining is also important in Poland. Copper, silver, sulfur, lead, coal, salt, and iron are all brought up from the ground. Poland is also one of the world's largest producers of feldspar, a mineral used in making glass and ceramics.

Poland has been famous for its amber for thousands of years. Much of it was found along the Baltic coast. Today, Poland produces about 12,000 tons of amber per year, in a variety of colors and shades. Poland's coal output is equally impressive at about 100 million tons per year.

What Poland Grows, Makes, and Mines

AGRICULTURE (2010)

Cow's milk	12,278,700 metric tons
Sugar beets	9,822,900 metric tons
Wheat	9,487,800 metric tons

MANUFACTURING

Food products (2010, value of sales)	US$43,625,000,000
Metal products (2010, value of sales)	US$16,543,500,000
Automobiles (2012)	647,803 units

MINING (2009)

Feldspar	550,000 metric tons
Copper	498,960 metric tons
Silver	1,206 metric tons

Poland has produced significant amounts of oil from time to time, and some Polish geologists believe there are still sizable strikes to be discovered. Most of the oil used in Poland, however, must be imported.

In recent years, Poland has also begun to use its hot underground waters to create geothermal energy, which could provide heat for more than thirty million homes.

Agriculture

Agriculture accounts for about 3.5 percent of the country's GDP and employs about 10 percent of the nation's workers. About one-third of Poland's land is suitable for farming, but only a fraction of it is actually used to grow crops or raise animals. While there are more than two million farms in Poland, most are relatively small—under 20 acres (8 hectares).

Leading farm products include wheat, rye, potatoes, sugar beets, oats, and barley. Dairy farms produce milk, cheese, and other products. Polish farmers also raise chickens, pigs, and beef cattle.

A man unloads a basket of potatoes at a farm in central Poland. Farmers in Poland grow about 8 million metric tons of potatoes every year.

Imports and Exports

As Poland's economy has expanded, so has its international trade. It is now one of the busiest trading nations in the European Union. About two-thirds of its exports, goods sold to other countries, go to other EU members. Germany accounts for about 26 percent of Polish exports. About 6 percent of exports go to the United Kingdom. France, the Czech Republic, Italy, the Netherlands, and Russia each take around 5 percent.

Heavy machinery and transport equipment are Poland's leading export items. This includes cars, trucks, and boats; smaller vehicles like golf carts and snowmobiles; and parts for manufacturers in other countries. Poland also exports a variety of electronics, including televisions, computers, telephones, and household appliances, as well as a small amount of furniture, medications, and beauty products.

Most of the imports, goods from other countries that are sold in Poland, are related to construction and manufacturing. Major imports include industrial machinery, transportation equipment, and chemical products. Few imports in Poland are intended for use by individuals or in the home.

Resources

- Potatoes and cereals
- Wheat
- Forests

- C Coal
- Cu Copper
- Fe Iron
- ⚒ Petroleum

Money Facts

The basic unit of currency in Poland is the zloty. It is divided into one hundred groszy (the singular is grosz). Coins have values of 1, 2, and 5 zloty and 1, 2, 5, 10, 20, and 50 groszy. Bills come in values of 10, 20, 50, 100, and 200 zloty. Each denomination of bill is a different size and color so they are easy to tell apart. The front of each bill has an image of a significant person from Polish history. The back shows a historical coin or symbol of Poland, such as the eagle or the coat of arms. For example, the 10-zloty note is predominantly brown and features Mieszko I, the nation's first ruler, on the front. The back shows a silver coin used during his reign. In 2013, 1 zloty equaled US$0.30, and US$1.00 was worth about 3.35 zloty.

About 25 percent of the imports in Poland come from Germany. Russia provides Poland with about 12 percent of its imports, and the Netherlands, China, France, and the Czech Republic each provide around 5 percent.

Transportation

Since joining the EU, Poland has worked to improve its transportation network. New expressways have been built across the country, and many other roads have been upgraded. Poland is also modernizing its rail network so trains can roll across the tracks at higher speeds.

The national airline is LOT Polish Airlines. It is the largest airline operating in central and eastern Europe. Poland's largest airport is the Warsaw Chopin Airport. The country also has major airports in Krakow, Gdansk, Wroclaw, and Poznan.

Poland has many seaports along the Baltic coast. The largest are in Szczecin, Gdansk, and Gdynia. From there, goods can be shipped around the world. Large passenger ferries also link Poland to Sweden, Finland, and other countries.

A large containership arrives at the port in **Gdansk. The city has been a major shipping and shipbuilding center for centuries.**

CHAPTER 7

The Polish People

THERE ARE ABOUT SIXTY MILLION POLISH PEOPLE in the world. About two-thirds of them live in Poland. Most of the remainder live in other European Union (EU) nations. When Poland joined the EU, many Poles went to other EU countries to work. More than a half million people born in Poland now live in the United Kingdom, and Polish is the second most common language spoken in England. Poles are also the largest ethnic minority in Ireland. The United States, Canada, and Brazil also have large Polish populations. In the late nineteenth and early twentieth centuries, an estimated one million Poles moved to the United States. Many settled in the New York City region or in the Midwest, particularly near Chicago, Illinois. Nearly six hundred thousand people in the United States speak Polish at home.

Opposite: **People performing traditional Polish folk dances often dress in colorful costumes.**

Polish Jews prior to World War II

Ethnic Poland

The great majority of people living in Poland—about 97 percent—are ethnically Polish. This is a fairly recent development. Before World War II, the Poland region was very diverse. But during the war, millions of Polish Jews were killed. The war also changed country borders and saw mass deportations and migrations. By the end of this turmoil, Poland was one of the least ethnically diverse countries in the world.

The largest ethnic minorities today are Germans, Belarusians, and Ukrainians. They tend to live near the country their ethnicity is associated with. Kashubians live near the Baltic Sea. Large numbers of a Polish-German minority group known as Silesians live in southwestern Poland. Some Silesians would like to become an independent nation. This historic region spills over from Poland into parts of Germany and the Czech Republic.

Ethnic Groups in Poland (2011 est.)	
Polish	36,000,000
Silesian	418,000
German	59,000
Belarusian	36,000
Ukrainian	37,000
Kashubian	17,000
Roma	12,000

Polish Language

The official language of Poland is Polish. Almost everyone who lives there speaks it. Polish is one of a group of languages called Slavic languages. In fact, it is the second most common Slavic language in the world after Russian, which has more than forty million speakers. While the majority of Polish

A sign in Poland along the Baltic Sea includes warnings in Polish (top), German, and English.

speakers live in Poland, there are also large numbers of Polish speakers in neighboring Belarus, Lithuania, and Ukraine.

There are four generally accepted dialects, or versions, of the Polish language, but they are all quite similar. Lesser Polish is commonly used in the southern part of the country. Greater Polish is more common in the west. Masovian can be heard in both the eastern and central areas, and Silesian is spoken in the southwest. Many people who speak Silesian believe that they belong to a distinct, separate culture and thus consider Silesian its own language, not a Polish dialect.

Pronouncing Polish

ą	like "o" in "own" (*dokąd* = where)
ci	like "chi" in "chip" (*cicho* = silence)
cz	like "ch" in "cherry" (*czerwony* = red)
dż	like "j" in "job" (*dżem* = jam)
dzi	like "gy" in "gym" (*dziura* = hole)
ę	like "e" in "hen" (*mogę* = I can)
ia	like "yu" in "yummy" (*miasto* = city)
ie	like "ye" in "yes" (*pies* = dog)
io	like "yo" in "yolk" (*Piotr* = Peter)
ł	like "w" in "wood" (*ładnie* = nicely)
ń	like "ny" as in "canyon" (*dzień* = day)
ó	like "u" in "bull" (*ból* = pain)
rz	like "j" in French "jour" (*rzeka* = river)
ś	like "sh" in "shift" (*śmiech* = laugh)
sz	like "sh" in "shift" (*szalony* = crazy)
zi, ż, ź	like "j" in French "jour" (*zima* = winter, *żurek* = a type of barley soup, *źle* = badly)

Common Polish Words and Phrases

Czesc	Hello
Do widzenia	Good-bye
Dzien dobry	Good morning
Dobry wieczor	Good evening
Bardzo dziekuje	Thank you very much
Nie ma za co	You're welcome
Milo Cie spotkac	Nice to meet you
Przepraszam	Excuse me (in order to pass by)
Ktora jest godzina?	What time is it?
Wesolych Swiat	Merry Christmas
Wszystkiego najlepszego z okazji urodzin	Happy birthday
Polska jest cudownym krajem	Poland is a wonderful country

The Goral dialect, spoken by the Goral people who live in the mountains of southern Poland, is more distinctive.

The Polish alphabet is based on the Latin alphabet used in the English-speaking world, but with a few notable differences. For one, several Polish letters exist in two forms, the second of each requiring the addition of a diacritical mark, such as an accent. For example, the *l* sounds like it does in English, but *ł* makes a *w* sound. The forms with and without the diacritical marks are considered separate letters. (In this book and many English-language publications, however, all letters are used without diacritical marks.)

Three letters in the English alphabet—*q*, *v*, and *x*—are used only in foreign words, so they are not part of the Polish alphabet. Subtracting these, the Polish alphabet has twenty-three consonants and nine vowels, for a total of thirty-two letters.

Living and Growing

Poland is home to more than thirty-eight million people. About 60 percent of the people live in cities. The Polish population has been declining in recent years. There are

A man in Poznan reads a Polish newspaper. In addition to the many Polish newspapers, there are also papers published in English and German in the country.

two reasons for this. The first is because many Poles have moved to other countries to work. The second is that Poland has a very low birthrate. In 2013, Polish women on average gave birth to just 1.3 children. That puts Poland at number 212 out of 224 countries on the scale of lowest birthrates in the world.

There are many reasons for Poland's declining birthrate. Many women are now going to college and having careers. Because of this, they put off having children until later in life, and sometimes decide not to have children at all. Many young people also worry about rising costs. Having children is expensive. Polish people point to the lack of government support of young families, and day care is hard to find. Moreover, women in Poland are not guaranteed their jobs back after they take time off to have a baby. As a result of the decline in births, today less than 15 percent of the people in Poland are fourteen years old or younger.

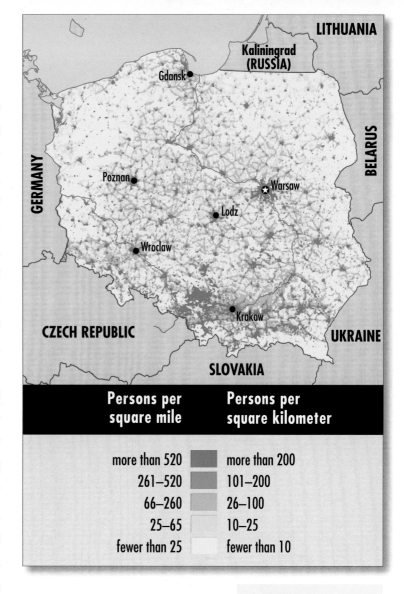

Persons per square mile	Persons per square kilometer
more than 520	more than 200
261–520	101–200
66–260	26–100
25–65	10–25
fewer than 25	fewer than 10

Population of Major Cities (2011 est.)

Warsaw	1,720,398
Krakow	759,137
Lodz	737,098
Wroclaw	631,235
Poznan	551,627
Gdansk	456,967

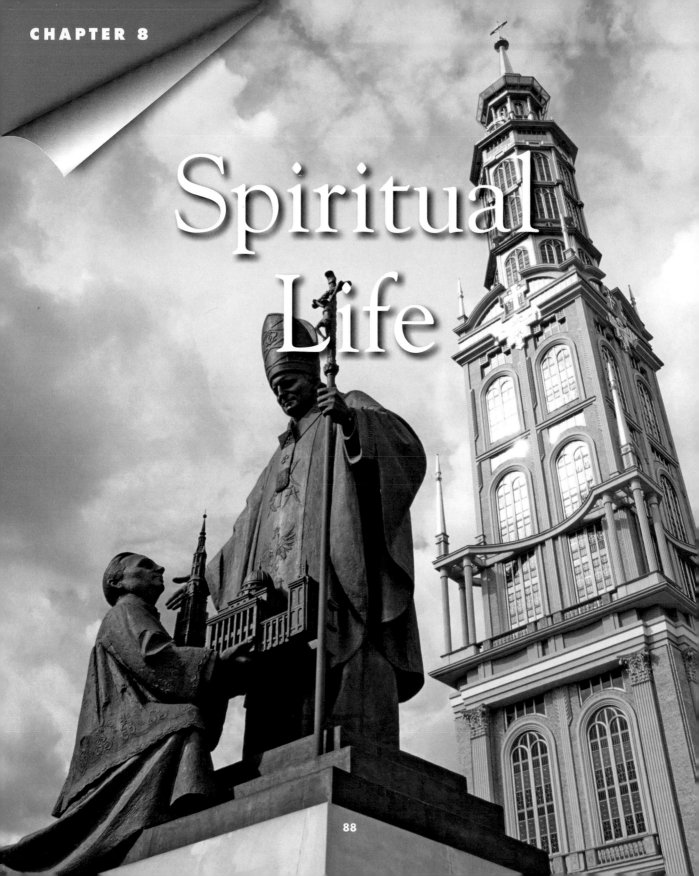

CHAPTER 8

Spiritual Life

MANY PEOPLE IN POLAND REGARD THEIR religious faith as central to their lives. They embrace it not just dutifully but enthusiastically. It is not unusual to enter a Polish home and find a large edition of the Bible displayed prominently alongside images of the Virgin Mary or Jesus Christ. Many Polish Catholics also keep photos and other images of Pope John Paul II. He was the first Pole to become pope, the leader of the Roman Catholic Church.

Opposite: **A statue of Pope John Paul II stands on the grounds of the cathedral in Lichen, Poland.**

Religion Today

Today, the overwhelming majority of Polish people belong to the Roman Catholic Church. Several hundred years ago, Poland was a mix of religious faiths. No one religion dominated. But by the eighteenth century, Catholicism had become the main Christian religion in Poland. Also, the mass slaughter of Polish Jews during World War II radically altered the religious makeup of the country. Prior to World War II, there were about three million Jews in Poland. Now, only about seven thousand remain. Most live in the city of Warsaw.

Although Catholicism is the dominant religion in the country, Poland's constitution provides for religious freedom for all people, regardless of their faith. Poland is home to members of Orthodox churches, and to many Protestants, including

A group of Muslims prays in Warsaw. An estimated thirty-one thousand Muslims live in Poland.

Jehovah's Witnesses, Pentecostals, and Seventh-Day Adventists, as well as Jews, Muslims, and members of many other faiths.

Worshippers fill a cathedral in Warsaw.

Catholic Life

Many Catholic Poles are deeply proud of their beliefs and hold the church in high esteem. Their faith helped them through difficult times.

Some Poles suffered religious persecution during the years of communist rule. The Soviet leadership claimed to be tolerant of religion in Poland, but many Poles still felt the need to worship in the privacy of their homes rather than attend public masses. It was not uncommon for people at meetings intended for other purposes—labor union gatherings, for example— to launch into prayer. Many Poles who lived through the

Religion in Poland (2012)	
Roman Catholic	91%
Orthodox	1%
Other	2%
Atheist/nonbeliever/ agnostic	5%
Not stated	1%

The First Polish Pope

Pope John Paul II was one of the most influential figures in Polish history. He was born Karol Jozef Wojtyla in the town of Wadowice in southern Poland on May 18, 1920, the youngest of three children. By the time he was twenty years old, his parents and siblings had all died. During World War II, he entered the priesthood. He became a bishop in 1958, and in 1967 he was elevated to cardinal, a senior position in the church. Elected pope in 1978, Wojtyla was the first non-Italian in more than 450 years to become pope. As pope, he chose to call himself John Paul II.

In the years that followed, John Paul II had a huge influence around the world. He improved relations between Christians, Jews, and Muslims. He inspired Catholics worldwide, traveling to more than 125 countries. Many of these countries had never been visited by a pope before.

John Paul was wounded in 1981 by a gunman named Mehmet Ali Agca. The pope visited Agca in prison a year and a half later to forgive him. John Paul II died on April 2, 2005. His funeral service at the Vatican drew more than four million mourners.

communist era maintain that their faith was one factor that fueled their determination to resist the oppression they faced.

When Karol Jozef Wojtyla became Pope John Paul II in 1978, Poles were tremendously proud. During his time as pope, the fervor for Catholicism in Poland increased.

In the Roman Catholic Church, the religious service is called a mass. Many Polish churches are packed during masses. In recent surveys, about half the Poles say they attend mass at least once a week.

A priest poses with children outside a church in Wadowice. The children have just made their first Communion, after which they can fully participate in the mass.

A Polish family prays before Christmas Eve dinner.

Most children in Poland receive religious education at home. Some schools do offer religious education, giving parents the option to include their children in the program.

Holidays

As a devotedly Catholic nation, Poland observes many religious holidays. Probably the most significant is Christmas, which celebrates the birth of Jesus Christ. Christmas in Poland is usually a three-day affair, starting on December 24, Christmas Eve. Polish families often decorate their Christmas trees on this day. The day ends with a magnificent feast. The meal begins with the breaking of bread called *oplatek*. Everyone eats a piece as a symbol of unity with Christ. This

Religious Holidays in Poland

Epiphany	January 6
Easter Sunday	March or April
Easter Monday	March or April
Pentecost Sunday	May or June
Feast of Corpus Christi	May or June
Assumption Day	August 15
All Saints' Day	November 1
Christmas	December 25

is followed by a dinner featuring a dozen different dishes, all without meat, to honor Christ's twelve apostles. Some of the more common dishes include fish, soups, and pastas.

A decorated Christmas tree brightens a square in Warsaw.

In some Polish homes, bits of hay decorate the table because, according to the Bible, Christ was born in a manger. Later, there is a midnight mass at the local church, which is decorated lavishly. The following day, people travel to the homes of family and friends and may attend a second church service. Although Poles do exchange gifts during the Christmas holiday, they place greater emphasis on family gatherings.

A priest in Lublin blesses food brought to a church on the day before Easter. Traditionally in Poland, people bring eggs, sausages, bread, salt, and pepper to church to be blessed.

Many churches continue to celebrate the Christmas season well into January. Christmas carols are sung at masses during this period.

Another significant religious holiday is Easter, which is the day that Jesus is believed to have risen from the dead. The Sunday on which Easter is observed varies, occurring in late March or April depending on the year. Easter in Poland has some of the same traditions as Easter in North America. Polish children delight in painting hard-boiled eggs in fanciful colors.

Poland also has some Easter traditions all its own. In some parts of the country, on the morning of Easter Monday, which is known as Smigus-Dyngus, boys are allowed to wake girls

In some places, Smigus-Dyngus is celebrated by people wearing traditional straw costumes, such as this man drenching a boy.

by dousing them with water. It is possible that this tradition stems from the symbolic ritual of purification with water in a spirit similar to baptism. Whatever the case, girls can sometimes get their revenge by performing the same ritual on the boys the following day. In some parts of Poland, girls can avoid their Monday soaking by paying a "ransom" of one or more of their brightly painted eggs.

The Basilica of Our Lady of Lichen is the largest church in Poland. It can hold twenty thousand worshippers.

Saint Ursula

One of Poland's newest saints is a woman who was born Julia Maria Ledochowska, on April 17, 1865. She was the fifth of ten children born into a wealthy family of both Polish and Swiss heritage. When the young woman became a nun in 1886, she took the name Maria Ursula.

In the early twentieth century, Ursula ventured into Saint Petersburg, Russia, to help establish a home for young Polish members of the Catholic Church. This was risky work because Catholicism was illegal in Russia then. Russian officials tolerated her for a time before forcing her to leave in 1914. From there she went to Sweden and began a school for girls, and then to Denmark to establish an orphanage. She returned to Poland in 1920 and began a congregation of nuns that specialized in providing services and educational opportunities to the poor.

Ursula died in 1939 at the age of seventy-four, and she was named a saint in 2003. Today, the congregation of nuns that she founded is active in twelve countries around the world.

Two other religious holidays take place during the late spring and summer months. The first, called Corpus Christi, is observed sixty days after Easter Sunday. It is a confirmation of the belief in Jesus Christ as the one true savior. Poles observe the Feast of Corpus Christi by attending a special Sunday service and enjoying a generous feast. Many Polish communities have public gatherings and processions. August 15 is Assumption Day, also known as the Assumption of Mary, which celebrates the Catholic belief that Mary, Jesus's mother, rose directly into heaven after her death.

Holy Places

To devout Catholics, some places are considered to have special religious significance. Religious people travel to these places on journeys called pilgrimages. One of the most popular pilgrimage sites in Poland is the Basilica of Our Lady of Lichen, in Lichen Stary, a village in central Poland. This village contains an image of the Virgin Mary that is said to have performed miracles. The

Jasna Gora Monastery in Czestochowa is even more popular. It holds a painting of the Virgin Mary and baby Jesus called the Black Madonna. It is said that Saint Luke made this painting on a cedar panel taken from the home of Jesus's family. The painting is called "black" because the paints have turned dark as they have aged. The Jasna Gora Monastery receives more than four million pilgrims every year.

Pilgrims pray in front of the Black Madonna in Jasna Gora Monastery. The painting is said to have been brought to Czestochowa in 1382.

Some Christian Poles also take time out for religious retreats. Put simply, a retreat is a break from the rigors of daily life to regain peace and calm as well as to reconnect with one's spirituality. In Christianity, the retreat is symbolic of the forty days Jesus is said to have spent alone in the desert. In modern times, Christians can take a retreat for any amount of time from a few hours to a few days. Sometimes they remain home; other times they travel to retreat sites. These retreats are like hotels in many ways, although they are usually in secluded areas and have a great emphasis on peace and contemplation.

In Poland, it is traditional to light candles and visit the graves of relatives on November 1, All Saints' Day.

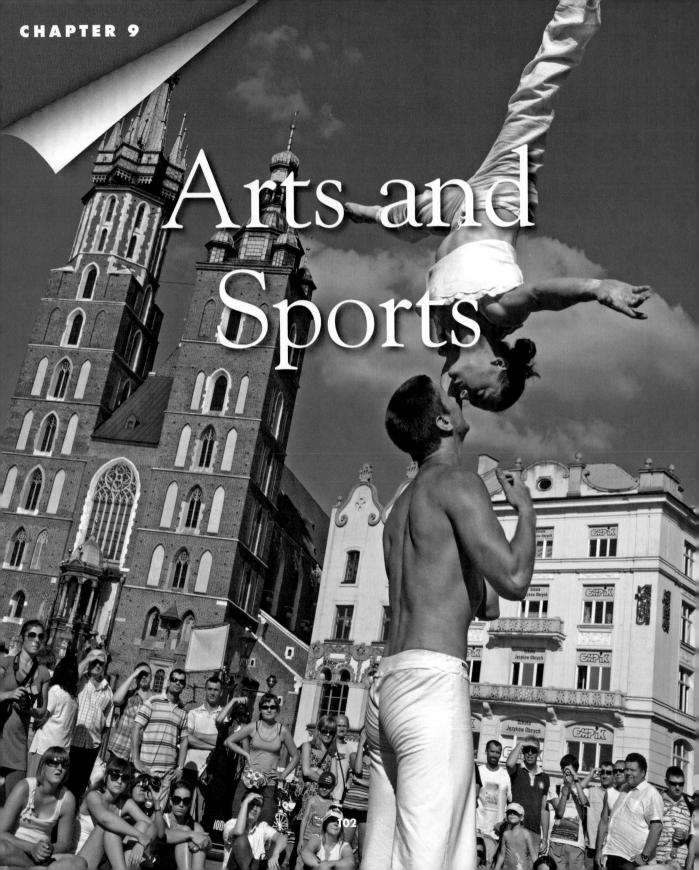

CHAPTER 9

Arts and Sports

POLAND'S STORYTELLING TRADITION DATES BACK thousands of years. The myths and legends told today have been handed down through the generations. Some of these stories attempt to explain how Poland evolved, while others focus on morality and humility.

One of the most popular myths is the tale of how the white eagle became Poland's national symbol. It begins with three brothers journeying into the wilderness to find new places to live. One of the brothers, Lech, found himself on the edge of a great lake. As he stood there, a huge, majestic eagle flew overhead, eventually landing in its nest high on a nearby rock. Lech was awestruck by the sight of the animal. When it spread its wings to take flight again, it appeared pure white against the brilliant red of the sun behind it. In that instant, Lech was so overwhelmed with emotion that he decided to build a village by the lake. That village was named Gniezno—"eagle's nest"—and it became Poland's first capital. Poland's first flag showed a white eagle against a field of red.

Opposite: **Acrobats perform at a festival in Krakow.**

Death of a Dragon

One well-known Polish legend explains how one of Poland's largest cities got its name. Many hundreds of years ago, there was a small village set near a hill. The village's older residents said that a dragon lived in a cave set into the hill, but the younger residents didn't believe in such things. A group of youngsters ventured into the cave one day, and to their surprise they found a dragon inside. The dragon was enraged that it had

been disturbed, and from that day on the villagers lived in constant fear. The dragon would sometimes venture into the village to destroy homes, eat farm animals, and sometimes even eat the villagers themselves. Attempts to kill the dragon only angered it further.

One day, a humble villager named Krakus came up with the idea of covering several sheep with a thick paste that would make the dragon thirsty. When the dragon ate the sheep, its thirst became so unbearable that it rushed to a nearby lake and kept drinking until it exploded. Krakus became a hero, and the village was renamed Krakow in his honor. Today, Krakow is the second-largest city in Poland. A statue of a fire-breathing dragon (left) stands outside Wawel Castle (above) to commemorate the legend. Nearby, in Wawel Hill, there is a deep cave that thousands of people visit every year to pay their respects to the clever Krakus.

Literature

For centuries, Polish literature has reflected the bitter challenges the Polish people have faced. The nation's writers have labored to communicate the hardships they have witnessed or experienced. Poland has produced some masterpieces by authors whose talent is matched only by their determination.

Poland has produced five winners of the Nobel Prize in Literature, the world's most prestigious literary prize. The first, Henryk Sienkiewicz, was awarded the prize in 1905. He wrote a series of epic novels about Polish history. Many of the novels of Wladyslaw Reymont, who won the Nobel Prize in 1924, concern the lives of everyday people. He is perhaps best remembered for his four-volume novel *Chlopi* (The Peasants) about the lives of peasants over the course of a year, which is written in the dialect of its peasant characters. Novelist Isaac Bashevis Singer grew up in Warsaw and became renowned for his depictions of Jewish life there. He moved to the United States in 1935 and was awarded the Nobel Prize in 1978. Poet Czeslaw Milosz received the prize in 1980 for his work, which explores Polish history and philosophy. Another poet, Wislawa Szymborska, won the award in 1996. Her work, which often concerns the details of everyday life, is noted for its precision and humanity.

Wladyslaw Reymont's best-known works include *Ziemia Obiecana* (The Promised Land). The novel, which describes life in Lodz during the industrial revolution, has been made into a movie twice.

Other Polish writers have also had a major impact. Adam Mickiewicz was a much-loved nineteenth-century poet who strived for Polish independence. Important twentieth-century writers include Witold Gombrowicz, a playwright whose work depicts absurd and extreme situations, and Stanislaw Lem, a science fiction writer renowned for his philosophical works about the limits of human communication.

Film

Poles have been making movies since the earliest days of cinema in the early twentieth century. In the 1950s, directors who

Nobel Laureate

Wislawa Szymborska was the first Polish woman to win the Nobel Prize in Literature. Szymborska was born in 1923 in the western Polish town of Prowent. During World War II, she worked on the railroads to keep a low profile and avoid Nazi harassment. It was at this time that the inspiration to write began. She tried publishing some of her early work after the war, but she could not get it past Soviet censors. Nevertheless, she embraced Soviet communist ideas at first and continued with her writing. By the mid-1960s, however, she had shifted her position on communism and began speaking out for more personal freedoms in Poland. From the 1980s onward, she became bolder in her public opposition to Soviet rule, and the themes in her poetry began to reflect not just her own dissatisfaction but also that of the wider Polish population. She was awarded the Nobel Prize in Literature in 1996, and continued writing until her death in 2012.

had studied at the Polish Film School in Lodz began making names for themselves. One of the greatest of these directors is Andrzej Wajda, whose work examines the trials of Polish society. His best-known works include *Ashes and Diamonds* (1958), *The Promised Land* (1975), and *Man of Iron* (1981), about the Solidarity movement. In 2000, Wajda received an honorary Oscar for his contribution to world cinema.

Another great Polish director, Krzysztof Kieslowski, drew acclaim for *The Decalogue* (1988), a series of ten short films, each one based on one of the Ten Commandments. He later drew international acclaim for his Three Colors trilogy—*Blue* (1993), *White* (1994), and *Red* (1994)—somewhat mystical films dealing with issues of morality.

Krzysztof Kieslowski's film *Blue* won the top award at the 1993 Venice Film Festival, one of the world's most prestigious festivals.

Agnieszka Holland directs films in both Poland and the United States. Many of her works touch on the issues of living under a communist government.

Agnieszka Holland has worked in both Poland and the United States. Her great European films include *Europa, Europa* (1990), about a Jewish teenager in Poland during World War II. She has also made English-language films such as *The Secret Garden* (1993), based on the classic children's novel about an isolated child who learns to enjoy the world.

Music

Poland has produced a distinctive type of music that developed in the 1500s. This music has its origins in folk music such as the mazurka, a lively dance in which couples stamp their feet and click their heels. A more formal waltz-style dance known as the polonaise (the French word for "Polish") also developed in this period. Composers took these traditional dances and incorporated them into their work. The great composer Frederic Chopin wrote many polonaises. He was born near Warsaw in 1810, and during his relatively short lifetime (he died at the age of thirty-nine), he wrote dozens of piano pieces that are still widely performed.

In the twentieth century, many of Poland's most talented musicians earned international acclaim. Pianist Ignacy Paderewski performed sold-out concerts around the globe but was also involved in politics and was named prime minister of the newly independent Poland after World War I. Arthur Rubinstein is considered one of the greatest pianists of the

Arthur Rubinstein continued giving concerts until he was eighty-nine years old. He died at age ninety-five.

twentieth century. Born in Lodz in 1887, he showed extraordinary skill at a young age and played in his debut concert at age seven. As an adult, he won particular praise for the way he played Chopin compositions.

Today, Poland is a fertile landscape for musical expression, with literally thousands of groups giving a distinctive Polish flavor to music in every genre, from rock and heavy metal to electronica and classical. Jazz is particularly popular, with musicians Tomasz Stanko, Michal Urbaniak, and others gaining international reputations.

Tomasz Stanko is both a trumpeter and a composer. He is one of the leading figures in Polish jazz.

The National Museum in Krakow

Poland's National Museum has several branches around the country. One of the greatest is located in Krakow. This branch has an impressive collection of more than 750,000 pieces of art, ranging from classical to modern, with photographs, paintings, and more. Construction of the main building began in the 1930s, but because of World War II and the difficult times after, it was not completed until the early 1990s. World War II led to another unfortunate consequence for the museum: Nazis looted the museum's collection, and many of the stolen pieces were never recovered. Aside from the paintings, the museum's current collection features sculptures, folk pieces, archaeological artifacts, furniture, clocks, musical instruments, and more. The museum has a particularly strong collection of recent Polish paintings, with important works by artists such as Jacek Malczewski and Stanislaw Wyspianski.

Visual Arts

The Polish visual arts have been heavily influenced by the nation's long struggle for independence. During the late nineteenth century, painters such as Jan Matejko made large, romantic paintings depicting events in Polish history. In the early twentieth century, the Young Poland movement introduced modern art to Poland. Stanislaw Wyspianski, a leading member of this movement, created paintings bathed in personal emotion. Jacek Malczewski, another member of this movement, focused on mythology and the fate of Poland.

In the years after World War II, Polish artists often expressed the misery of their people, with muscular and

Magdalena Abakanowicz created her sculpture *Unrecognized* between 2001 and 2002. The work consists of 112 figures, each nearly 7 feet (2.1 m) tall.

dramatic paintings designed to speak directly to the public. National and religious symbols began to reappear in a more forthright manner during the 1980s, reflecting the spirit of the Solidarity movement. More recently, Polish artists have worked in a full range of modern art. The works of modern artist Magdalena Abakanowicz includes sculptures of groups of oversized human figures. She uses different materials, including metal, burlap, and wood, to achieve an eerie, disturbing effect with her creations.

Sports

Sports are hugely popular in Poland. The most popular sport in the country is soccer, known as football in much of the world. The Polish national team won the Olympic gold medal in soccer in 1972 and the silver medal in 1976 and 1992.

Professional teams draw huge crowds in Poland, and many people play on school or community teams.

Motorsports are also tremendously popular in Poland. The most popular event is known as Speedway. This is a competition between four or six motorcyclists on an oval track. The motorcycles use just one gear and have no brakes, and the riders circle the track four times. The track itself is flat and usually made of dirt or pulverized shale. In the turns, the riders are not so much accelerating as they are sliding, and the challenge is to

Speedway motorcyclists race around a track in Torun, in northern Poland.

Marcin Gortat, a center for the Phoenix Suns, dunks the ball during a game against Memphis. In 2013, he was the only Pole playing in the National Basketball Association.

simply control the vehicle and remain upright. Speedway has been practiced in Poland since the 1930s. The top Speedway events have the highest attendance numbers of any spectator sport in the country. The best riders represent Poland on the national team, which has won many world championships.

Another popular sport in Poland is basketball. The top Polish league is known as the Tauron Basket Liga (TBL), which was founded in 1995 and today consists of twelve teams. In the 1960s, Poland's basketball team was one of the finest in the world, competing in the Olympics and other international competitions and winning several medals. The game has enjoyed a resurgence in popularity in recent years, and Poland hosted the European Basketball Championship in 2009. Poland also has a long tradition of women's basketball. The Polska Liga Koszykowki Kobiet, the top female basketball league in the nation, was formed in 1929. The women's national team has an impressive record in international competition, having most recently won the gold medal in the European Women Basketball Championship in 1999.

Volleyball is another of Poland's most enthusiastically supported sports. Both the men's and the women's national teams are among the most successful in the world. The men's team, for example, was ranked in the top ten in the world from 1998 until 2010 and won the European Championship in 2009. The women's team has been no less impressive, winning medals in the Olympic games in the 1960s and winning the European championship in 2003 and 2005.

Volleyball is also a popular casual sport. It is played in schools and community leagues, and at festivals and family gatherings. Whenever the weather is nice, Poles often head outside for a volleyball game.

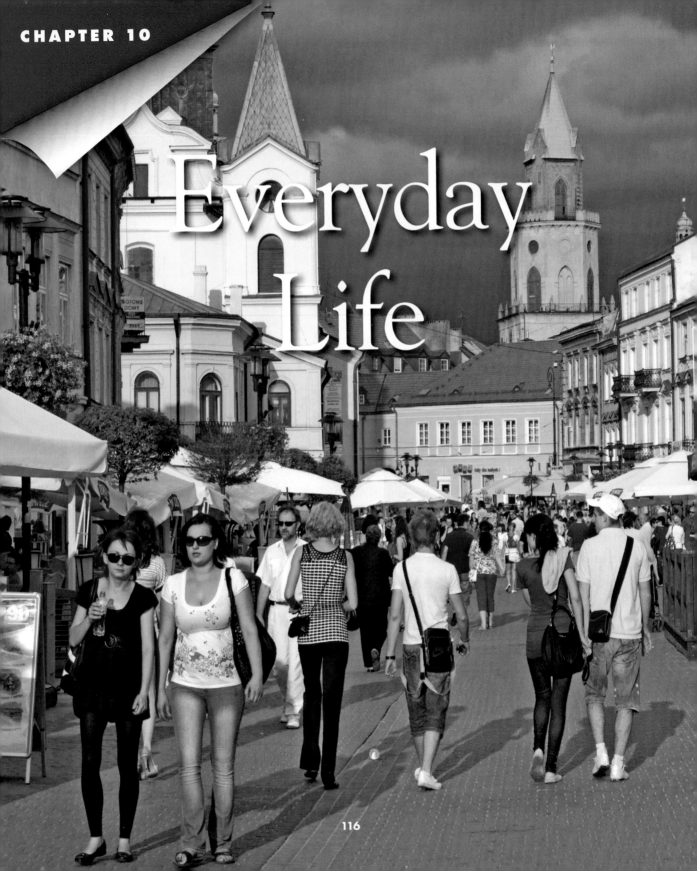

CHAPTER 10

Everyday Life

POLAND'S DIFFICULT PAST HAS BRED IN THE POLISH people an admirable determination. Many Poles also seem to have a natural cheerfulness and optimism. They are open and friendly, living with a hearty joyfulness, while also viewing the world with a certain caution and a well-grounded sense of reality. They are proud of their Polish identity. And while they do not forget the past, many look hopefully toward the future, as their nation's economy continues to strengthen and Poland becomes an ever more powerful part of the European Union.

Opposite: **People fill the streets of Lublin, in southeastern Poland.**

Getting By

While Poland's economy has made drastic improvements since the 1990s, many challenges for ordinary families still remain. With the increased demand for consumer products, for example, prices are rising faster than salaries, forcing

A group of college students relaxes in Wroclaw. In Poland, more women than men go to college.

families to pinch pennies. The average middle-class family in Poland spends about a quarter to a third of its income on food alone. Having children is risky, not just because of the costs, but also because many women fear being fired from their jobs or not being hired in the first place if they even express an interest in starting a family sometime in the future.

Jobs are sometimes difficult to find. The unemployment rate among younger people entering the workforce is particularly high. Many people immediately move back in with their parents after graduating from college. They live there, sometimes for years, waiting for a good job opportunity.

Health Care

Generally, the better off people are, the longer they live. As Poland's economy has improved in recent decades, the average life span in Poland has increased. Today, Polish men can expect to live to age seventy-three, while women have an average life expectancy of eighty-one. Many Poles have started paying more attention to their health, focusing on eating well, getting exercise, and quitting smoking.

The government pays for health care for all Polish citizens. This includes all operations and extended hospital stays. Some people, however, choose to seek private care, which they pay for themselves. In Poland, some physicians will make house calls, going to the patient's home, but this is an expensive service.

An elderly man bicycles through Rzeczyca, in central Poland. About one in seven Poles is over the age of sixty-five.

Elementary schools in Poland have an average of eighteen children per class.

Education

For the average Polish child, schooling is much the same as it is in the United States and Canada. From preschool, which starts at the age of six, until the end of ninth grade, children attend classes from September until the end of June. The subjects they study are similar to those studied in North America. Children study math, science, reading, Polish, foreign languages such as English or German, geography, history, and more. They get a brief lunch period in the middle of the day when they can sit and talk with their friends, and then a

Playing Zoska

Zoska is a simple game that has been enjoyed by Polish children for generations. It is similar to the American game of hacky sack but with an added twist. Two or more people can play zoska at one time. Each player draws a circle around himself or herself in the dirt or on the pavement with chalk. Then the players pass the zoska, a ball like a hacky sack, to each other by using any part of their bodies except their hands. Players can hit the zoska while it is still in the air or catch it on some part of the body and then pass it along. However, players can't let it touch the ground in their circles, or else they'll lose a point. Before the game begins, players agree on how many points a person can lose before being out. When only one person is not out, that person is the winner.

recess period where many will take up a game of soccer or basketball. Private and Catholic schools usually require uniforms, but public schools do not.

Schoolboys kick around a soccer ball in Poznan.

After ninth grade, children either go to high school, known as *liceum*, for three years, or learn a trade in the Polish equivalent of a vocational school, known as a *technikum*. Liceum is the preferred path for those planning to go on to college.

Jagiellonian University, formerly known as University of Krakow, is the oldest university in Poland. It was founded in 1364. Other prominent universities include University of Warsaw, Adam Mickiewicz University in Poznan, and Catholic University of Lublin.

A Polish woman prepares mushrooms for a soup. Traditional Polish food tends to be hearty.

Good Food

The people of Poland take great pride in the foods of their country. Meats such as beef, pork, and chicken play a large role in many of their recipes. They also use a broad selection of spices. Cabbage is the most common vegetable, although potatoes, cucumbers, tomatoes, beets, and mushrooms are also used frequently. Soups are extremely popular. Polish specialties tend to be rich and use a lot of eggs, butter, cream, and cheeses. Poles are also very fond of rich desserts, with pastries being among their favorites. A traditional Polish meal can take many hours to prepare.

Kielbasa, a type of sausage, is one of the best-known Polish dishes. It can be prepared smoked or unsmoked, and made with beef, pork, chicken, veal, turkey, lamb, or a combination of these meats. It is spiced to individual tastes and formed into many different shapes and sizes. Most kielbasas are made in a very large tubular form—much larger than the average American hot dog. Kielbasa can be boiled, baked, smoked, or grilled, and then is served alone or on a bun, with onions, peppers, cabbage (sauerkraut), and garlic. Kielbasa is also included in some soups, and it is sometimes eaten cold as an appetizer, cut in disks and served with toothpicks.

Kielbasa and ham are two of the most popular types of meat eaten in Poland.

Kielbasa Soup

Kielbasa is one of the most popular foods in Poland. Have an adult help you make this soup filled with kielbasa sausage.

Ingredients

2 tablespoons butter

1½ pounds kielbasa, sliced

1 cup onion, chopped

2 cups celery, chopped

4 cups cabbage, chopped

2 cups carrots, sliced

1 bay leaf

½ teaspoon dried thyme

2 tablespoons white vinegar

3 cups beef broth

2 cups water

3 cups potatoes, cut into cubes

Salt and pepper

Fresh dill, chopped

Directions

Melt the butter in a large skillet. Add the sausage, onions, and celery, and cook over medium heat until the sausage is lightly browned. Pour this mixture into a large pot, and add the cabbage, carrots, bay leaf, thyme, vinegar, broth, and water. Bring the contents of the pot to a boil, reduce the heat, cover, and simmer for 1 hour. Add the potatoes to the soup, and cook until they are tender. Season with salt and pepper. After the soup is ladled into bowls, put a bit of chopped dill on top as a garnish. Enjoy this soup with fresh bread.

Pierogi are another common Polish dish. They are small dumplings filled with meat, cheese, or ground potato, and often sauerkraut as well. Some cooks include a variety of vegetables such as onions, mushrooms, peppers, and spinach. The best pierogi are made by hand, dropped into boiling water, and then finished in a hot skillet to give the outside a brown crispiness. Because they are relatively easy and inexpensive to make, they originated in the homes of poor Polish people. It wasn't long, however, before even Polish royals began to enjoy them. Today, there are popular dessert versions, substituting the meat-and-potatoes filling for fruits such as blueberry, peach, cherry, raspberry, strawberry, and apple. Powdered sugar is sometimes dusted over the top, and a variety of syrups and jams can be used for dipping.

Pierogi have been a favorite Polish food for centuries.

Celebrations

Many Polish holidays are religious, but Poles celebrate many national holidays throughout the year as well. Two of the biggest holidays celebrate Poland's independence.

May 3, Constitution Day, honors the creation of the Polish constitution of 1791, the first constitution in Europe. Although this constitution was in effect for only a short time, it stood as a symbol of the desire for Polish independence. Today, Constitution Day is celebrated with parades streaming down the streets of Polish cities, politicians giving speeches, music playing, and cannons blasting.

A band marches in a parade in Warsaw on Constitution Day.

A young boy waves Polish flags during a ceremony marking Polish Independence Day.

November 11 is Polish Independence Day. It marks the end of World War I, when Poland again became an independent nation. It is celebrated with family get-togethers, concerts, and parades. It is a day for Poland to be proud.

National Holidays

New Year's Day	January 1
Epiphany	January 6
Easter Sunday	March or April
Easter Monday	March or April
Labor Day	May 1
Constitution Day	May 3
Pentecost Sunday	May or June
Corpus Christi	May or June
Assumption of the Blessed Virgin Mary	August 15
All Saints' Day	November 1
Independence Day	November 11
Christmas Day	December 25
Boxing Day	December 26

Timeline

POLISH HISTORY		WORLD HISTORY	
Modern humans begin building settlements in what is now Poland.	8000 to 6000 BCE		
		ca. 2500 BCE	The Egyptians build the pyramids and the Sphinx in Giza.
		ca. 563 BCE	The Buddha is born in India.
		313 CE	The Roman emperor Constantine legalizes Christianity.
Slavonic tribes arrive in the Poland region.	500s CE		
		610	The Prophet Muhammad begins preaching a new religion called Islam.
The Polan people rise to power.	900s		
Mieszko I becomes a Christian, bringing Christianity to Poland.	966		
		1054	The Eastern (Orthodox) and Western (Roman Catholic) Churches break apart.
		1095	The Crusades begin.
		1215	King John seals the Magna Carta.
		1300s	The Renaissance begins in Italy.
		1347	The plague sweeps through Europe.
Queen Jadwiga of Poland marries Jagiello of Lithuania, uniting the two countries.	1386		
Poles and Lithuanians defeat the Teutonic Knights in the Battle of Tannenberg.	1410		
		1453	Ottoman Turks capture Constantinople, conquering the Byzantine Empire.
		1492	Columbus arrives in North America.
		1500s	Reformers break away from the Catholic Church, and Protestantism is born.
The Polish-Lithuanian Commonwealth is formed.	1569		
Russia, Austria, and Prussia begin to partition Poland.	1772		
		1776	The U.S. Declaration of Independence is signed.
Poland creates the first constitution in Europe.	1791		

POLISH HISTORY		WORLD HISTORY
		1789 The French Revolution begins.
Poland ceases to exist with a third partition.	**1795**	
Poles rebel against the Russians in the November Uprising.	**1830**	
		1865 The American Civil War ends.
		1879 The first practical lightbulb is invented.
		1914 World War I begins.
Poland becomes independent.	**1918**	**1917** The Bolshevik Revolution brings communism to Russia.
		1929 A worldwide economic depression begins.
Germany invades Poland on September 1; the Soviet Union invades Poland on September 17.	**1939**	**1939** World War II begins.
Jews in the Warsaw Ghetto stage an uprising.	**1943**	
		1945 World War II ends.
		1969 Humans land on the Moon.
Poles riot over high food prices.	**1970s**	
		1975 The Vietnam War ends.
Karol Wojtyla becomes Pope John Paul II.	**1978**	
Trade unions form a group called Solidarity and demand greater freedom.	**1980**	
		1989 The Berlin Wall is torn down as communism crumbles in Eastern Europe.
Solidarity leader Lech Walesa is elected president.	**1990**	
		1991 The Soviet Union breaks into separate states.
		2001 Terrorists attack the World Trade Center in New York City and the Pentagon near Washington, D.C.
Poland joins the European Union.	**2004**	**2004** A tsunami in the Indian Ocean destroys coastlines in Africa, India, and Southeast Asia.
		2008 The United States elects its first African American president.
President Lech Kaczynski and other leaders are killed in a plane crash.	**2010**	

Fast Facts

Official name: Republic of Poland

Capital: Warsaw

Official language: Polish

Warsaw

National flag

Southern Poland

Official religion:	None
National anthem:	"Mazurek Dabrowskiego" ("Poland Is Not Yet Lost")
Type of government:	Parliamentary republic
Head of state:	President
Head of government:	Prime minister
Area of country:	120,726 square miles (312,679 sq km)
Latitude and longitude of Warsaw:	52°13' N, 21°00' E
Bordering countries:	Russia to the northeast; Lithuania, Belarus, and Ukraine to the east; Slovakia and the Czech Republic to the south; and Germany to the west
Highest elevation:	Mount Rysy, 8,199 feet (2,499 m) above sea level
Lowest elevation:	Raczki Elblaskie in the Vistula Lagoon, 6 feet (1.8 m) below sea level
Average daily high temperature:	In Warsaw, 30°F (–1°C) in January, 75°F (24°C) in July
Average daily low temperature:	In Warsaw, 21°F (–6°C) in January, 59°F (15°C) in July
Average annual precipitation:	19 inches (48 cm) in Warsaw

Krakow

Currency

National population (2013 est.):	38,383,809	
Population of major cities (2011 est.):	Warsaw	1,720,398
	Krakow	759,137
	Lodz	737,098
	Wroclaw	631,235
	Poznan	551,627

Landmarks:
- ▶ ***Bialowieza Forest***, Bialystok
- ▶ ***Biebrza National Park***, Goniadz
- ▶ ***Museum of Art***, Lodz
- ▶ ***Old Town***, Krakow
- ▶ ***Wawel Castle***, Krakow

Economy: Poland's economy is growing rapidly. Service industries such as accounting, banking, and software design are thriving. Poland also has a robust manufacturing sector. The nation produces industrial machinery, ships, automobiles, furniture, food products, chemicals, glass, paper, textiles, and much more. Lead, silver, copper, sulfur, coal, salt, and iron are all mined in Poland. The nation's leading agricultural products include wheat, rye, potatoes, sugar beets, oats, barley, and milk.

Currency: The zloty. In 2013, 1 zloty equaled US$0.30.

System of weights and measures: Metric system

Literacy rate (2012): 99.5%

Schoolchildren

Justyna Kowalczyk

Common Polish words and phrases:

Czesc	Hello
Do widzenia	Good-bye
Dzien dobry	Good morning
Dobry wieczor	Good evening
Bardzo dziekuje	Thank you very much
Nie ma za co	You're welcome
Milo Cie spotkac	Nice to meet you

Prominent Poles:

Frederic Chopin (1810–1849)
Pianist and composer

Nicolaus Copernicus (1473–1543)
Scientist

Marie Curie (1867–1934)
Chemist and two-time Nobel Prize winner

John Paul II (1920–2005)
Pope

Tadeusz Kosciuszko (1746–1817)
General and statesman

Justyna Kowalczyk (1983–)
Skier

Czeslaw Milosz (1911–2004)
Nobel Prize–winning poet

Arthur Rubinstein (1887–1982)
Pianist

Wislawa Szymborska (1923–2012)
Nobel Prize–winning poet

Lech Walesa (1943–)
Leader of the Solidarity movement and president

To Find Out More

Books

▶ Altman, Linda Jacobs. *The Warsaw Ghetto Uprising: Striking a Blow Against the Nazis.* Berkeley Heights, NJ: Enslow, 2012.

▶ Docalavich, Heather, and Shaina C. Indovino. *Poland.* Broomall, PA: Mason Crest, 2012.

▶ Pavlovic, Zoran. *Poland.* New York: Chelsea House, 2008.

DVDs

▶ *Invitation to Poland.* Polart, 2002.

▶ *Krakow, Poland.* Travel Video, 2009.

▶ *Poland Rediscovered: Krakow, Auschwitz and Warsaw.* Back Door Productions, 2004.

▶ *A Promise to My Father.* Syndicado, 2013.

▶ Visit this Scholastic Web site for more information on Poland:
www.factsfornow.scholastic.com
Enter the keyword **Poland**

Index

Page numbers in *italics*
indicate illustrations.

Warsz, 62
Wawel Castle, 22, 104, *104*
wetlands, 19, 28, *28*, 29, 32
white eagle (national symbol), 30,
    30, 103
wildflowers, 34, *34*
wild hamsters, 29
wildlife. *See* amphibian life; animal
    life; insect life; marine life; plant
    life; reptilian life.
women, 87, 114, 115, 118, *118*
World War I, 46
World War II
    concentration camps, 49
    death camps, 49, *49*
    deportations and, 49, 50, 82
    Germany and, 9–10, 48, *48*
    ghettos, 49–50, *50*
    Jewish people and, 9, 10, 49, 82,
        90, 108
    John Paul II and, 92
    Krakow and, 22

Lodz and, 22
map of, *51*
National Museum and, 111
Soviet Union and, *11*, 48, 49
underground fighters, 50–51
Warsaw and, *48*, 49–50, *50*, 51, 62
Wislawa Szymborska and, 106
Wroclaw, *14*, 22, *22*, *54*, *70*, *79*, 87,
    118
Wybicki, Jozef Rufin, 67
Wyspianski, Stanislaw, 111

Y
Young Poland art movement, 111

Z
Ziemia Obiecana (Wladyslaw
    Reymont), 105
zloty (currency), 78, *78*
zoos, 31, 32, *32*
zoska (game), 121

Meet the Author

WIL MARA IS AN AWARD-WINNING AUTHOR OF more than 140 books, many of them educational titles for children. He began writing in the late 1980s with several nonfiction titles about herpetology. He branched out into fiction in the mid-1990s when he wrote five of the popular Boxcar Children mysteries. He has since authored more than a dozen novels, including *Wave*, which was the recipient of the 2005 New Jersey Notable Book Award, *The Gemini Virus*, and *Frame 232*.

Photo Credits

Photographs ©: